The WOODEN BOAT

The WOODEN BOAT

· ● ·

Joseph Gribbins

FRIEDMAN/FAIRFAX

A FRIEDMAN/FAIRFAX BOOK

©1996 by Michael Friedman Publishing Group, Inc.

First Paperback Edition 2001

Please visit our website: www.metrobooks.com

Library of Congress Cataloging-in-Publication Data available upon request.

ISBN 1-58663-223-X

Editor: Sharyn Rosart
Art Director: Lynne Yeamans
Designer: Stephanie Bart-Horvath
Photography Editor: Emilya Naymark

Color separations by Bright Arts Graphics (S) Pte Ltd
Printed in China by Leefung-Asco Printers Ltd.

3 5 7 9 10 8 6 4 2

Distributed by Sterling Publishing Company, Inc.
387 Park Avenue South
New York, NY 10016
Distributed in Canada by Sterling Publishing
Canadian Manda Group
One Atlantic Avenue, Suite 105
Toronto, Ontario, Canada M6K 3E7
Distributed in Australia by
Capricorn Link (Australia) Pty, Ltd.
P.O. Box 704, Windsor, NSW 2756 Australia

To the summer residents of Scudders Falls, New Jersey, whose wooden boats gave me such pleasure as a boy.

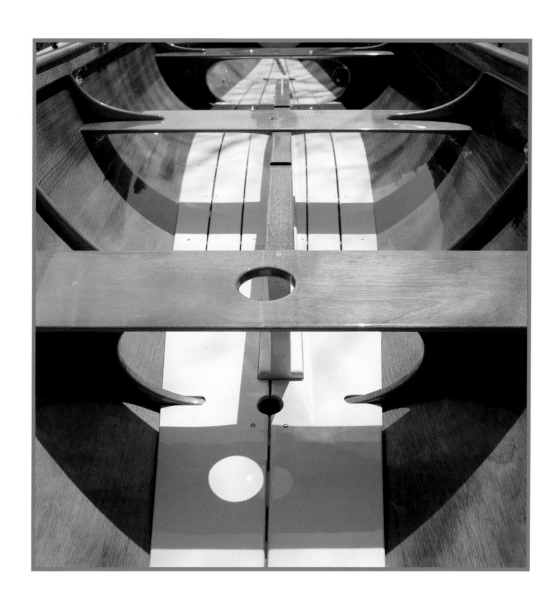

CONTENTS

· · · · · · · · · · · · · · ●· · · · · · · · · · · · · ·

CHAPTER 1

Something Magical, Something Essential

A large part of the magic in most wooden boats is their beauty. Wood has such richness of finish, such sculptural potential, so much ability to be worked with subtlety, and maybe even a sort of soul that few other materials even come close. It is hard to imagine furniture made out of anything else, even though some of it is metal or plastic. It is hard to imagine boats made out of anything else, although some boats are metal and plastic. There is a place for metal and plastic. We would find a wooden refrigerator somewhat odd. Even a wooden tugboat looks wrong, just as wooden railroad cars that were built during wartime shortages of metal looked wrong.

But wood is the stuff for elegant small boats and bigger yachts, for dining tables and bedsteads and canoes. It seems an essential material for things made with art as well as with artifice. Wood's beauty and suitability for the work are a large part of a wooden boat's magic, and a large part of the essence of a good wooden boat is its equilibrium of proportion and structure, fit and finish, shape and weight, straight line and curve. You can see and sense that poise and rightness in most of the boats we see in this book, and there is something very satisfying in the experience. These things look right; they look beautiful; they are essential; and they are magical.

Something else that attracts us to wooden boats—inside, underneath, or prefacing all such exalted stuff as spectacular sweeps of sheerline or plate-glass varnish—is the nice reality that these are things people have made with their hands and with relatively simple tools. There is hand-eye coordination in it. There are sometimes mistakes and compromises. There is worry. There is sweat. There is living and human involvement in every inch of a wooden boat.

A wooden boat begins as an idea in the designer's or the craftsman's head. Sometimes the idea is worked out on paper, and sometimes an existing model is modified to suit the new scheme right on the shop floor, using eye and instinct, those essential design tools. In the old days, designers and builders whittled half-hull models, turning and sighting along the miniature

Above: A wooden vessel takes shape in a boatyard on the coast of Maine—here with frames set up on the keel. Very few parts of any ship or small boat have straight lines.

Page 8: Long varnished deck, brass fittings, leather upholstery, slim white hull—a perfect blend of style and substance is this Fay and Bowen launch.

boat-to-be and sculpting more carefully until things looked just right. The model was then used to scale up the full-size lines. These days, designers and builders often use a computer program to manipulate the lines of a boat until the result matches what's in their heads and in their dreams.

Once the dream has been defined, the material begins to be gathered. Bronze bolts, brass screws, Honduras mahogany, cotton canvas, oak, cedar—all this natural stuff is a pleasure to work with. The craftsman

enjoys his work—and there is often more to it than that. As British author and small-boat connoisseur Arthur Ransome once wrote: "The desire to build a boat is one of those that cannot be resisted. It begins as a little cloud on a serene horizon. It ends by covering the whole sky, so that you can think of nothing else. You must build to regain your freedom." Meanwhile, the boat gains its freedom. Here is what Adirondack guideboat builder Steve Kaulback had to say about the process of boatbuilding: "I like to think of myself as not really building the boat but

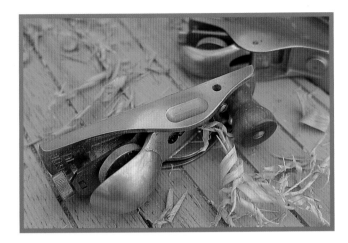

rather giving direction and advice to the boat as it builds itself. I create the conditions necessary for construction to take place, and my hands are present while the hull is formed or a fair curve is determined, but the boat has a life of its own."

This may sound somewhat sacramental, yet it expresses the tactile and spiritual satisfactions of wooden

boatbuilding. Even a boxy skiff, nailed and screwed together from white pine household lumber, is the fulfillment of a dream, the transformation of boards into something aesthetically pleasing, the result of satisfying work with wood.

The work begins when the boat's backbone is shaped and set up—keel, stem, deadwood, transom. Molds that match the shapes that the boat's ribs will soon take are installed on the keel and made true with eye, plumb line, and measuring tape. When flexible battens, called ribbands, are sprung around the molds, the shape of the boat is revealed. The hull's ribs are steamed and bent to shape, or frames are sawn and otherwise constructed, often from curves and crooks that a tree formed in its growing. Frames go in and are soon supplemented by floor timbers,

Careful workmanship and tight joints are evident even in a small boat like this one, with its steam-bent oak ribs and cedar-strip planking.

*L*apstrake pulling boats reach the finishing stage in the boatshop of the Maine Maritime Museum, one of many places all over the world where the art of wooden boatbuilding is kept alive.

deck beams, gunwales, inwales, or whatever the type of boat requires. Then planking is shaped and fastened to this strong skeleton. When the last plank is hung, the hull is complete. Decking, seating, ceilings, bulkheads, or whatever else the design requires follows until the boat is all there, all raw wood, shiny new hardware, and fastenings. What could be more satisfying than seeing this subtle thing take shape from the lumber pile and the hardware gathered on the workbench?

How much to paint and how much to finish bright are tough decisions. A canvas deck will be painted. The boat's bottom will get paint, maybe antifouling paint, and perhaps a contrasting waterline stripe. The right combination of painted surface with oiled or varnished wood is a matter of aesthetics. The truth is that nearly any choice will be good. A working vessel or a knockaround skiff may be all paintwork. It may be all paintwork in almost all one color, such as soft grey with dark blue trim, or light tan with brick red and a bit of green. A creamy white inside, a glossy black outside, a copper-green bottom, a white stripe along the waterline—there are too many good choices. A strip-built canoe or a mahogany run-

A *Concordia yawl with a varnished African-mahogany hull sails the Maine coast. The price of this much beauty is many hours of skilled boatyard labor.*

*C*ertain harbors have become
havens for wooden boats, their
owners, their admirers, and, perhaps
most important, their fixers. This
boatyard, which is peopled by skilled
wood repairers and refinishers, is in
Sausalito, California, on San
Francisco Bay.

T his red rowing skiff is proof that plain paint, sometimes in a vivid color, can be the right choice for a small wooden boat.

about may look just right with almost all the wood gleaming under multiple coats of varnish. But a little paint—a thin red waterline stripe on the canoe or a white bottom and bright blue waterline stripe on the runabout—will always enhance the brightwork with some contrast. Even wild or otherwise unconservative paint schemes may be appropriate. Small boats always look good in chrome yellow, express-wagon red, and electric blue.

What you have when the last lick of paint has dried is something magical and essential, something to make you smile. The builder smiles as much as the customer when the boat is delivered, although he may feel some

postpartum pain. Time to get busy on another boat. The customer smiles as he puts the boat through its paces on his own piece of water. Friends and guests smile as they admire his good taste and good luck. You smile as you see the photos of these boats in this book. There is something here that attracts us all. It is certainly magical. It is certainly essential in the sense that something vibrates between who we are and what the boat may be or represent. It may be the shape of the boat, the beauty of the wood or the finish, the thought of cruising or fishing in this boat, or the satisfaction of having it around for the odd moment or hour of use.

A perfectly restored gas-engine launch from the beginning of the twentieth century shows off her bright paintwork and one-cylinder engine.

Varnish is the finishing touch for most wooden yachts, as the deck of this 1950s Chris-Craft cruiser demonstrates. The white caulking lines are traditional—and somewhat theatrical.

Wooden boats are frequently a blend of separate sculptural elements. Here is a synthesis of varnished-wood hull, chrome-and-glass windshield, and plastic-grip steering wheel.

A more subtle part of the attraction to these boats, and less easy to touch than their physical beauty or utility, is their association with the past. Rowing a small boat or paddling a canoe on a lake or river out of sight of houses and highways, you feel like an Indian, a voyageur, or Huckleberry Finn in his skiff. Getting on the water is getting in touch with a different reality, and part of the journey in a traditional boat can be imagining that your experience is the same experience someone had in a boat decades or centuries before. And maybe it is. The voyageurs exploring the Great Lakes three hundred years

ago may have fantasized they were Vikings in the same spirit that we in our canoes imagine we are voyageurs.

In our very different world of unnatural materials and, let us be honest, not-so-natural lifestyles, it is not particularly easy to experience the past or even to imagine it especially well. But we can get in touch with a reality much like that of the real or imagined past when we go aboard a traditional small boat, and once again there is something very satisfying in the experience. What a refreshing change to trade places with a 1920s yachtsman, a Gold Cup competitor, or Thoreau and his brother on a rowing excursion in the summer of 1839, even if it is only for an hour or two.

We romanticize the past—which is to say we enjoy having a romance with it. It shapes itself in our imaginations just the way we want it. It may be that imagining or remembering the jolly and successful past is one way to make it happen again. On a boating excursion, it is certainly a way to enhance the experience, a way to forget blisters and wet feet and that we left the lunches in the car.

And so we enjoy and cherish our traditional small boats and classic yachts, vehicles of romance, ego, and soul satisfaction, beautiful to look at, sometimes exciting and sometimes just comforting to use. Some of us even enjoy the maintenance attention that wood and paint and varnish require. Presented in the following pages are close to a hundred good examples of wooden boats that range from dinghies to luxury yachts. They are magical, essential, and—best of all—numerous. The revival of interest in wooden boats of all kinds continues to resurrect the old ones, to create new ones based on old models, to refine traditions, and to bring fresh ideas to the ancient craft of shaping wood into boats. There are hundreds of thousands of wonderful wooden boats in this world, and more all the time.

*S*ince the 1960s, gatherings of wooden yachts and boats have taken place all over the world. This boat parade in Southern California features schooners in the background and a Dutch botterjacht with tanbark sails in the foreground.

At an antique-and-classic boat gathering, a perfect Chris-Craft barrelback shows off the blend of varnished wood and chrome trim that is characteristic of speedboats from the 1940s and 1950s.

CHAPTER 2

Something Troublesome, Something Natural

When I was a little boy, our summer cottage on the Delaware River had three boats—two rowboats of obscure origin and an Old Town wood-and-canvas canoe. One of the rowboats was a classic cross-planked flatiron skiff with no decorative touches except for the nice shape of the aft seat, which had the traditional curlicues at each end. The other rowboat, also cross-planked and made from lumberyard pine, was a flat-ended punt exactly like the boats used by Pogo and Albert Alligator in American comic strips. Each of the rowboats was about twelve feet (3.6m) long, and the canoe was a little longer. None of these boats had names.

In the late spring, my father would give the two rowboats a cursory scraping and sanding and then a coat of green glossy paint. It was the same paint he used on flower boxes, picnic tables, and the floor of the gazebo that overlooked the river. The painting and scraping, which took place one dry and sunny weekend in between leaf-raking, was done right on the saw-horses on the lawn where the two boats had spent the winter. The canoe was

kept under the porch and didn't need fresh paint or varnish for years. Anyway, it didn't get any, and the varnished inside, which had once had a golden glow, was dark and dull with age and old varnish by the time I came along.

My sister and I played in these boats every summer. They served as a bridge over the mud along the shore, leading us to cleaner footing in slightly deeper water with stones on the bottom. They became rafts when anchored in water deep enough for diving. They were vehicles for trips to an island a hundred feet (30.4m) away, sometimes with my mother and a picnic lunch aboard. They were platforms for fishing, at anchor in the evening with both fish and mosquitoes biting. I learned to row those boats when I was six or seven, and I used them and sometimes the canoe in later years to go all the way across the river and explore the woods and another island on the Pennsylvania side. I took with me an Army Signal Corps knapsack, boy-size, which held two peanut butter sandwiches and a sling-shot. I did not wear a personal flotation device.

Opposite:

Expanses of varnish and perfect
paintwork distinguish this vintage
cruiser—a blend of pleasing design,
craftsmanship with wood, and lots of
attention to maintenance.

Below:

Wooden sailing dinghies like these
are boats for the simpler pleasures of
being on the water. They have an
appropriately simple beauty.

When I was twelve, my summer friend George, whose family had another cottage along our stretch of the river, was given a twelve-foot (3.6m) Thompson cedar-strip outboard boat with a fifteen-horsepower Evinrude engine. The whole package was put together by Jimmy Abbott and his Titusville boat dealership, which was located in a barn behind his house. George and I used it for expeditions up the river to see more boats and more boat activity, including the adventures of a group of boys my age. They had a shack in the woods and their own docks, complete with little plywood speedboats their fathers had built from kits or from plans in *Mechanix*

Illustrated. After a whole summer of riding around in a real powerboat, I had to have an outboard boat of my own.

The next spring, with $75 of my own money, I bought a twelve-foot (3.6m) Chris-Craft plywood runabout that had been built from a kit by my friend Joel Sykes. Joel was two years older and had built the boat in his family's garage across the street when he was twelve or thirteen. He had done it perfectly, giving it beautiful decks and seats of varnished mahogany-faced plywood. It had a forward deck, a forward cockpit, a center deck, an after cockpit, and small side decks that became wider aft as they met the transom. It was the little speedboat of my

Maintenance is a large part of wooden-boat ownership. Here a woman is caulking the seams of an old sailing yacht using ancient and specialized tools—and ancient and special skills as well.

dreams. My father took me to a Mercury dealer, who supplied me with a seven-and-a-half-horsepower Merc engine and a red steering wheel. I installed the steering wheel so that I drove from the after cockpit (kneeling down like the outboard-racing heroes I followed in *Boat Sport* magazine). The boat had golden decks of varnished Philippine mahogany, white topsides, a bright red bottom, that red steering wheel, light gray insides, and the green Mercury motor that I wiped down with motor oil to enhance the shine. The whole outfit was beautiful. It was also nearly as fast as George's fifteen-horsepower bathtub of cedar.

After a few years, the boys up the river at Jacob's Creek had their fathers build them real Class B outboard racing boats from plans and kits—boats that had more powerful Mercury ten-horsepower, sixteen-horsepower, and even twenty-horsepower motors on their transoms.

Some wooden-boat owners and restorers enjoy the work as much as the play. Maintenance can be recreational, and repairing the gunwale of a small boat like this one is easy and satisfying.

All curves, all sculpture—this new copy of a traditional sailing yacht design is ready for the planking and decking that will cover its bones.

One of these boats was built by its sixteen-year-old owner and finished with its mahogany-plywood sides varnished and its lovely pointed nose painted with red flames, hot-rod style. It was a great boat, a synthesis of several themes from the 1950s in New Jersey—home boatbuilding, stock outboard racing, and the teenage culture of oily hair, hot rods, a pack of Luckies rolled up in the sleeve of your T-shirt, and a sense that anything was possible.

Those were happy days indeed on our five-mile (8km) stretch of the Delaware, every weekend full of boats, water-skiers, fishermen alongshore, and, for me, the glamorous activities of the guys up the river with their floating street rods. In the summer of 1955, I found a damaged outboard racing boat at a marine dealer's yard

downriver and bought it for $80. I bought a used Mercury Mark 20 a week later from the same dealer for $150. I had been working in a supermarket that winter and spring, and I had a lot of money. My father and I repaired the boat, and I painted it red in the after half and white in the forward, with a diagonal division of the colors that shot the white part aft like spray flying. This was a 1930s airplane paint scheme that I copied from another boat I had seen on the river. It looked wonderful.

George and I played with our little speedboats for a few summers before we went away to college. George ordered a center deck with a steering wheel from the Thompson Boat Company. We installed it one June day in his backyard, where he kept the boat upside down on sawhorses, the same way my father stored his nondescript rowing skiffs. My own boat was not neglected. I built seats for the front cockpit, and using whatever paint came to hand, I worked up some new and interesting paint scheme every year. One design had abstract red flames on a white background. I remember riding my awful J.C. Higgins bicycle up to our cottage and back, five miles (8km) each way, to do some of the presummer sanding and varnishing.

When George and I went off to college and changed our lives forever, our boats deteriorated while we flourished in the greater world. My father gave my boat and motor to a family up the road because their son-in-law was interested in it. He wasn't interested enough, and the father of the bride, clearing out the garage, floated the boat down the river. I never found out what happened to the Mercury Mark 20. George's boat was put on sawhorses under a walnut tree at his family's summer cottage, and someone gave it extra protection by throwing a canvas tarp over it. Moisture under the tarp was continual, as were summer rot spores and winter freezes. One day I checked on George's boat and poked my finger through the bottom. The cedar had turned to mush. All those boats are gone now; they are gone so utterly that nobody now can tell where they went. They disappeared within a span of ten years, and there was nothing unusual about it. Wooden boats in the 1950s were disposable.

This long preface to a discussion of the peculiarities and problems of wooden-boat ownership is, I think, a necessary background to the chapter's promise of some-

Lovely in every detail, a lapstrake rowing skiff peeks out from behind a piling, ready for a pull around the harbor or a picnic trip to a nearby beach. Simple boats like this one are vehicles for such simple pleasures, and such simple pleasures may also include scraping and painting.

A Maine marina full of wooden yachts and a few larger vessels—tourist schooners under cover—gets ready for the short but intense summer season Down East.

thing troublesome and something natural. Simply put, the something troublesome is that wooden boats are things that deteriorate over time, just as we do. This is something natural and, I am pretty sure, unavoidable. Another something troublesome is the obsession with perfection that seems to have come along since the wooden boat revival of the 1960s and 1970s. This is natural, too, and really something to be celebrated. This book is nothing less than a celebration of wooden boats at their most exalted.

I am struck by the contrast of how easy and unobsessive working on boats seemed back then and how different it seems today. I think of my father contentedly slapping paint onto those nondescript rowboats (he loved to paint things, as I do), or my bike trips at age fifteen to devote an hour of casual labor to a little boat. I remember the small bit of preseason varnishing and fussing that George and I did, and the fact that all those boats spent winters outside on sawhorses. In my memories of those boats and their use, they never seemed to deteriorate or lose their shine. Well, hardly ever. I recall the high price of a foot-square (929 sq cm) piece of Honduras mahogany purchased for one summer's repairs—so there were repairs, but only a few. I do not think that I am romanticizing or even simplifying the past. These were fairly new boats, after all, and to our teenage eyes they were beautiful and perfect.

In 1975, I took over the family summer cottage along with my wife, our daughter, and our two sons. Under one

of the several decks built by my father was an eight-foot (2.4m) plywood-and-mahogany rowing dinghy. It had been left there by a neighbor boy who had gone off to college. Anybody who asked could keep a boat on my father's little waterfront, and this was one of them. We pulled it out, hosed it off, and discovered odd bits of rot in the plywood. The mahogany seats, bow piece, and transom were great-looking slabs of Central American mahogany in fine condition. My guess is that the boat was built from a kit shortly after World War II, when such stuff was cheap.

I rebuilt the boat for my two boys, who were then eleven and fourteen. But it wouldn't do to just patch up the rot any which way and throw some paint on it. I found some comparable plywood and cut out the rot spots in neat squares. I glued in matching squares of new wood. I fiberglassed the outside of the boat and carefully filled and sanded the edges of the patches on the inside. I then painted the outside navy blue and the inside a nice buff. I also sanded the old finish off the mahogany seats, the inside of the transom, and the bow piece, and then I gave them four coats of spar varnish. It took more than a month of evenings and weekends to achieve all this, and the boys lost some time they might have had on the water, but this is the way I thought the job needed to be done in 1975. By that summer, I had seen a lot of perfect boats in magazines and at antique boat shows, and perfection—or something darn near it—was my goal. I also enjoyed every minute of the work.

When all the painting, varnishing, and fixing is done, what you have come summer is the lap of luxury.

I still have this little boat. It has been rebuilt a number of times, receiving new topsides of very expensive African-mahogany plywood, oak inwales that were new in 1979 and are starting to deteriorate, and very fancy sheer strakes made from pine lattice. Every year I fix and rebuild and refinish this little boat. Every year I suffer the wisdom of my sons. "Why don't you just build a new one?" they say. Two years ago, while moving the boat around the yard, my wife and my older son pulled the bow piece loose from the sides. "I'll build you a new one!" my son announced. He's a professional carpenter. I calmed him down and explained that I enjoyed sticking the boat back together every spring and making it look as nice as possible. I enjoy it with the knowledge that some spring the boat won't be the same anymore: eventually no part of the original boat will be left, or, possibly, neither boat nor owner will be able to make the trip to the Connecticut River. It's a ritual and a game for me, but the little boat must look as good as it can. At this point, I would never be able to just throw a coat of paint on it

Wooden boats deserve wooden boathouses. These two boathouses on Canada's Lake Rosseau creatively accommodate daysailing boats.

over a weekend as my father thought nothing of doing. My father did not have the perverse perfectionist influence of things like *Wooden Boat* magazine or this book.

There are other boats. A year after I rebuilt the little derelict for the boys, I bought my older son a Lincoln fiberglass canoe, which he wanted; and for my younger son I acquired from a friend a Class B outboard racing boat, which the twelve-year-old wasn't sure he wanted. Well, he'd find out; I'd had one like it when I was a kid. We paddled the canoe home from the dealer's, and we did a test run with the little speedboat, which had a fifteen-horsepower Mercury motor. Both were satisfactory experiences. The Class B outboard racing boat was a 1951

Sid-Craft that had set a speed record of just under fifty miles per hour (80kph) with a ten-horsepower Mercury racing motor in 1952.

We still have this boat. It was originally owned by Jim Coulbourn, a hero of 1950s outboard racing in New Jersey. The boat has been given several refinishings over the years, including new mahogany-plywood decks and padded vinyl seats. Next year it will get a new bottom. The forty-five-year-old marine plywood is finally delaminating, and without a doubt it has quantities of rot in its core. The boat may get a new paint scheme along with the new wood. It is now bright blue with a white racing number and with golden varnished mahogany and mahogany-faced plywood on the deck and inside.

There are two other wooden boats that were acquired with the idea that a little bit of work would make them perfect. One is a seventeen-foot (5.1m) Penn Yan sea skiff with a sixty-five-horsepower Mercury motor. In 1965, the boat, the motor, and the trailer were bought new in Islamorada, Florida. They then went to Candlewood Lake in Connecticut, then to Lake Champlain in Vermont, and finally to Duxbury, Massachusetts, near where I bought the whole outfit at a neighborhood yard sale in 1974. The other boat is an exquisite seventeen-foot (5.1m) lapstrake outboard runabout. It was built in the Thousand Islands in 1958 from Honduras mahogany, wood that was possibly appropriated from the Hutchinson Boat Works, where the man who built it had a day job. I bought that one in 1987.

This Fish Class sloop, which was designed by the great Nathanael Herreshoff, is a classic daysailer dating from 1914. She is shown here sailing in, appropriately, the annual Classic Yacht Regatta in Newport, Rhode Island.

*T*he tourist schooners that sail the coast of Maine every summer are among the larger wooden vessels that have survived time and the end of their careers of catching fish or carrying cargo.

I have never put either of these boats in the water. The sea skiff has had its topsides and insides scraped and repainted, and its motor has had $500 worth of rehabilitation, but the boat is not yet ready to be seen and admired by the waterfront public. Maybe next year, when the mahogany seats have been taken down to the wood, restained, and given five or six coats of varnish, and when the mahogany windshield frame is rebuilt and refinished again. How to get the glass back in the windshield and replace the now-deteriorated rubber that holds the glass in place is one of the problems to be solved.

One difficulty with the one-of-a-kind and extremely beautiful Thousand Islands runabout is that it needs its wood to swell tight to make it leakproof, something that hasn't been done to it for eighteen years. The runabout needs to be sunk to the gunwales for a few weeks in some nontidal water, in a place where children won't play in it and vandals won't vandalize it. It also needs to have its decks taken down to the wood, restained, revarnished, and given fresh new white lines all over the place—those theatrical caulking lines that no respectable mahogany runabout can appear in public without. Maybe I'll do it next year. I plan to take a week off in the spring. Perhaps the weather report will promise dry days. Perhaps there will be no fires to put out at work or at home. Perhaps I'll be able to do it all in a week.

I comfort myself in this situation of laziness, distraction, false hope, genuine love for these boats, and guilt and responsibility for their fates—and, let us not forget, their exaltation—with the thought that they are now stabilized. They have not been burned, sent down the river, left to rot, given sloppy coats of paint, or filled with dirt and planted with petunias.

Next summer the two little boats will go into the Connecticut River looking as good as new, or nearly so. The two bigger boats will continue their evolution to perfection—possibly with more haste but always with joy in the work: sanding a nice piece of mahogany and laying down a golden skin of spar varnish; filling dings and scratches in painted wood with auto-body paste, then sanding and repainting the wood with enamel that flows off the brush like a liquid mirror; perhaps cutting out a dark and rotted section of wood and replacing it with so perfect a match that only close inspection will show the surgery.

The wooden boats in this book are testaments to those kinds of activities, to the labors of restoration professionals and amateur hackers, to the satisfactions inherent in their work, to the beauty and craftsmanship these boats represented when they were new and continue to represent with caring ownership, and to the perfectionism that is both the joy and the curse of loving them so much.

They are worth the effort. Wooden boats are some of the great handmade objects in the long history of our uniquely human ability to coordinate hand and eye, mind and spirit.

Classic yachts like this Alerion replica being sailed in a brisk breeze gather annually on the first weekend of September in Newport, Rhode Island, for the Classic Yacht Regatta.

CHAPTER 3

Traditional Small Boats

Small-boat traditions in America and in much of Europe go back less than two hundred years. Before the 1800s, "small" boats were small in contrast to fishing smacks and lighters and larger vessels, but their construction was muscular compared to the many finer and lighter boats that came along in the nineteenth century. We can see this difference in drawings of boats from the 1740s and the 1840s. Many eighteenth-century small boats were built like miniature ships. They were built to withstand hard use, to serve as working-class rather than leisure-class vehicles, and perhaps as smaller examples of the shipbuilding standards and techniques that shaped their bigger sisters—thick ribs and planking, depth and capacity of hull, mass and weight. Except for proportion, construction standards do not seem to have altered very much from ship to boat, especially for boats that were used around ships and on the coast.

The nautical world is very conservative. Nothing changes quickly, and old traditions are revered. The small boats of the 1700s in Europe and America were not very different from those of centuries before. We could label them ancient small boats and not be far from the truth. These were working boats—lighters, ship's boats, and vehicles for fishermen—and by the beginning of the nineteenth century there were forces in play that would transform them.

New ideas and new boats came along in a new century that believed in progress on a variety of fronts, most of them technological. On the waterfront, new technology was accompanied by the idea that little boats were beautiful, interesting, and fun. This idea came from classes of people who had the time and the money to pursue what we now call sport. The new small boats of the nineteenth century are the boats we now identify as traditional small boats. On the technical front, they are firmly in our own time's traditions of stronger and lighter engineering, and on what we might call the social front, they are vehicles for getting on the water for pleasure rather than for labor.

Shown here under construction (above) and under sail (opposite) is Daisy, a twelve-foot-six-inch (3.8m) skiff designed by Harry Bryan and built by students at the Wooden Boat School in Brooklin, Maine.

lously evolved into the wood-and-Dacron ultralight rowboat of the 1990s. If this keeps up we may see the old wherry achieve boat nirvana as some gossamer creation that can row, sail, fly, and maybe disappear.

The evolution of small boats from ancient and heavy to fine and light in the nineteenth century is clear. It is less clear why this happened. Recreational use of small boats is almost certainly a big factor. The heavy rowboat capable of carrying a load and being banged around, the boat that three or four fishermen might wrestle off the shore and then row a mile or two (1.6 to 3.2km) to the fishing grounds, or the maid-of-all-work that two representatives of a chandlery would overload and row very carefully to a ship at anchor in the harbor—these were not the boats that two sports and their ladies (or two ladies and their sports) would row on a Sunday afternoon to take the air and visit a distant sandspit for a picnic.

For most of these rowing and paddling boats, the evolution during the past two hundred years has been from heavy and structured to light and simple, an evolution that continues and can be seen in the contrast between the traditional small boats in this chapter and the untraditional examples in the next. The untraditional small boats are often the traditional types reborn and rethought in new materials—and made lighter and simpler. The heavy wherry of the eighteenth century became the Whitehall boat of the nineteenth century, then miracu-

Another factor in the rapid and creative evolution of the small boats that we now consider classics must have been the corresponding evolution of tools and machinery. The years between 1760 and 1860 brought us the Industrial Revolution, that dramatic shift from rural and handmade to metropolitan and machine-made. Wooden boats have always been handmade, but technological innovations—such as machine-milled lumber and a greater variety and availability of woodworking machinery, hand tools, and mass-produced fastenings and hardware—changed both the craft and the business of boatbuilding. And they transformed the boats.

One of the great freshwater classics is the Adirondack guide-boat. An extremely light rowing boat, it was developed in the last half of the nineteenth century for fishing and hunting on the lakes and streams of the Adirondack region of New York State.

Coastal and harbor boats had the most dramatic evolution in the nineteenth century. They were sturdier and heavier than they needed to be, and for social or technological reasons they had nowhere to go but to lighter and finer forms while remaining almost as sturdy. Boats for lakes and rivers were already built light as vessels that either lived in easier weather and water conditions or were one-person vehicles. During the last century, as they evolved on the Thames or the Seine or in the Adirondacks, these became lighter and finer, too.

The Thames River skiff, a fine-lined lapstrake adaptation of heavier wherries with a distinctive Viking look (which makes anybody who sees one suspect fairly direct Norse lineage), evolved on England's great boating river. The New England dory, a workingman's boat made from a few broad planks, was developed from the *bateaux* that served French fur traders in the 1700s. This simple boat then became an all-purpose vehicle for both sides in the French and Indian War, and later began to be built from Boston to Newfoundland as a cheap and capacious little

A similar exercise in a lightweight rowing boat, with some modern details, is this double-ended dory with a sliding seat, developed and built by Lowell's Boat Shop of Amesbury, Massachusetts.

*T*he adaptable dory is a simple boat with a flat bottom and flared sides. Here is a sailing dory with a small cabin developed by Lowell's Boat Shop.

boat for the fisheries. It then became the boat of choice for woodsmen on their log drives down the rivers, and it finally took shape as an elegant little boat that gentlemen raced for sport in the 1920s and 1930s on the North Shore of Boston.

The Whitehall boat, a legendary and influential type, evolved from the ship's boats of the eighteenth and early nineteenth centuries. In the first half of the 1800s, these small boats became as characteristic of the New York waterfront as gondolas are of Venice. The Whitehall,

named for Whitehall Street in lower Manhattan, was a lovely transom-sterned small rowboat, originally lapstrake but later smooth-planked. It was used in old New York as a water taxi, chandler's delivery boat, and crimp's vehicle (to be loaded with drunk or otherwise incapacitated candidates for a long sea voyage, who were rowed out to a ship that was ready to sail and needed more crew), as well as for other harbor errands. The much-admired Whitehall began to be built in other ports, from Boston to, eventually, San Francisco. It was refined all

Left:

Also a product of Lowell's Boat Shop is this dory configuration, a rowing skiff with sliding seat.

Below:

A detail of the Lowell Boat Shop's sailing dory.

Pete Culler's Good Little Skiff—a so-called flatiron skiff—was designed in the 1950s as a utilitarian little boat for sailing or rowing, and also for easy construction by backyard boatbuilders. As a type, the flatiron skiff goes back at least through most of the nineteenth century in America.

during the nineteenth century by builders and their working or sporting customers, and individual boats were often fitted with sailing rigs or made in ultralight racing versions. The Whitehall also influenced the shapes of a variety of regional rowing boats in the United States and overseas.

People built small boats at home in the nineteenth century, and the boats they built tended to be what we now call skiffs—simple vehicles with flat bottoms, transom sterns, nails for fastenings, and household pine or cedar for material. Skiffs, we can recall, were the favored stolen or found transportation for Huckleberry Finn in his adventures. Like the Whitehall and the dory, types and variations of skiffs migrated all over the country from beginnings that are obscure but probably European. And like the Whitehalls, skiffs came in brawny and

ultralight versions, as they still do. We show a few of them in these pages, including Pete Culler's classic and sturdy Good Little Skiff, and Steve Redmond's more recent Whisp, an elegant little boat.

When Europeans came to New England they were introduced to the canoe, a boat type they had never seen before. They learned how to build and use these versatile paddling boats from the Native Americans, and over time they created their own versions. The Chesapeake Bay log canoe, once a fisherman's boat that was literally carved from two or three logs pinned together, is now a racing sailboat. Other log canoes or dugouts were used on the waterfronts of the East Coast, including huge dugouts that served the oyster fishery around New Haven, Connecticut, in the nineteenth century.

Another recent variation on the flatiron skiff is Steve Redmond's Whisp, a deliberately lightweight and elegant little boat, and another design intended for home boatbuilding.

J. Henry Rushton of Canton, New York, designed and built legendary sailing, rowing, and paddling boats during the great years of Adirondack fishing, hunting, and canoeing. This boat is one of his delicate, decked sailing canoes from the 1890s.

It was the birch-bark canoe of Canadian and New England Indians that had the greatest influence and evolution. In the last half of the nineteenth century, sportsmen in England adopted the canoe form for beautiful double-paddle boats made from cedar or mahogany, and these canoes, with decks and all-varnish finish, were taken on camping and exploring trips all over the world. The English decked canoe migrated back to America, where J. Henry Rushton of Canton, New York, built the best of them in the Adirondacks. Rushton canoes are valuable antiques now, and replicas are being built. The open canoe with upswept ends that we identify as a "canoe" came along near the end of the nineteenth century as a cedar-strip version of the birch-bark canoe with a tough hide of painted canvas. A handy and unfussy way

A detail from one of Rushton's creations.

Perhaps the most familiar and popular small boat in the world is the open canvas-covered cedar canoe. This is a replica of an early E.M. White canoe built by the Island Falls Canoe Company of Dover-Foxcroft, Maine.

to get out on the water, the open canoe is almost certainly the most popular small boat in the world.

A twentieth-century contribution to the traditional small boat fleet is the one-design sailboat. Small sailboats for racing go back before the Civil War in America, and some notable early examples are the sandbaggers and the tuckups that working watermen built and raced on the weekends, sometimes for big cash wagers, as a kind of bus-

man's holiday. In this century, fleets of boats were designed and built with the exact same measurements for yacht clubs, sailing clubs, and groups of unaffiliated sailors who wanted to race similar or identical boats. This meant that sailing skill rather than design or construction tricks would decide the winner. These were one-design boats, and the idea was so sensible and so popular that there are now more than three hundred classes of small (less than

Canoelike in form, but with a simple spiritsail and decks that surround the cockpit, the Delaware Ducker was developed on the lower Delaware River in the nineteenth century as a nimble vehicle for bird shooting.

thirty feet [9.1m]) sailboats that compete in local fleets in nearly every part of the world. Before the 1960s, nearly all of these boats were wood. Many still are, and some people remain true to the idea that small sailboats should be built in the family garage by those who sail them—an old-fashioned notion in our time of more money, less leisure time, and fleets of fiberglass boats produced in factories.

Traditional small boats range from the primordial canoe to the spruce-and-plywood one-designs of the 1930s and 1940s. They are the products of constant thinking about how to get across the water with more speed, more carrying capacity, more stability, more durability, and perhaps more style—with each element varying according to the needs and home waters of the oarsman, paddler, and sailor. They are descendents of centuries of such evolutions in technique and enjoyment. They are more than just little boats. They are inspired and inspiring inventions, works of art and craftsmanship, and objects of great satisfaction to their owners.

Note: Sources for plans, patterns, kits, and completed boats are given in an appendix at the back of the book.

▶
▶
▶
▶
▶ **S**hown opposite, top, and at left
▶ is one of the world's great traditional
▶ small sailboats—the Herreshoff
▶ 12½, built by the Herreshoff
▶ Manufacturing Co. About 450
▶ were built between 1914 and 1943,
▶ and most of them have survived.
▶ The varnished little boat on page
▶ 52, bottom, is another Herreshoff
▶ classic— a lapstrake dinghy.

CHAPTER 4

Untraditional Small Boats

New materials or new applications of familiar materials have traditionally given us new boats. The twentieth century brought us very thin veneers of boatbuilding woods, such as cedars and various mahoganies, able to be layered up in almost any shape: hot-molded if stuck together with resin or glue under heat and pressure, or cold-molded if made into boats at normal temperatures with epoxy as the adhesive. Epoxy resins—super-strong, gap-filling, and easy to use—have encouraged experimentation with ever-lighter skins of wood glued together with epoxy and then finished with more epoxy to enhance strength, durability, and longevity. A 1980s phenomenon was the canoe or small rowing boat with a frame of spruce and ash, a skin of Dacron cloth, and a weight of less than twenty pounds (9kg). Another twentieth-century material is what we now call plywood. Plywood has been with us in some form or another for more than a century. It was particularly popular for small wooden boats during the explosion of interest in boating and home boatbuilding that occurred after World War II. This

interest in wooden boats lasted through the 1950s until fiberglass became the dominant boatbuilding material in the United States and Europe during the 1960s.

Plywood has been one of the materials of choice for experimenters building untraditional small boats since at least the 1930s. One of the great small-boat geniuses of our time, or any other, was C. Raymond Hunt, the inventor of the deep-vee hull form that is now the running surface of nearly every powerboat in the world. In 1938, Hunt had his friends Bob Pierce and Dick Fisher build him a twenty-four-foot by four-foot-two-inch by two-foot-six-inch (7.3 by 1.2 by 0.7m) hull from sheets of plywood as a design experiment for a lively racing sailboat that could be built economically by home-builders or commercial shops. Hunt's International 110 was a technical success and eventually a racing success, with fleets from Boston to Seattle to the Philippines (although it looked less like a boat than a coffin). The 110 was one of our time's first untraditional small boats—an alien con-

*T*he 110 Class sloop, with its coffinlike design, was one of this century's first untraditional small boats. Above and on page 54 are 110 Class sloops racing. On page 55, a detail from one of these racers.

ception when compared with other one-design sloops—and it still seems radical nearly sixty years after the first 110 was launched. In the years after World War II, Hunt followed this experiment with a thirty-foot (9.1m) 210, a thirty-six-foot (11m) 410, and a forty-four-foot (13.4m) 510, although he softened the looks and behavior of these boats by giving them canoe-form hulls and less severe lines.

A successor to Ray Hunt in plywood boatbuilding experiments is Philip C. Bolger, a Gloucester, Massachusetts, author and boat designer who has made a specialty of what he and his boatbuilding partner Harold "Dynamite" Payson call Instant Boats. Phil Bolger designs these dead-simple plywood creations, and Dynamite Payson builds the prototypes and modifies them when necessary to create the easiest possible projects for ama-

Two of Phil Bolger and Harold Payson's Instant Boats—the boxy Turtle (foreground) and the Zephyr, with its clipper bow (background). Both have been designed for ultra-simple construction by amateur boatbuilders.

teurs. There are limitations to plywood—principally the inability of its flat sheets to take sophisticated, rounded shapes—but the great advantage of the material for experimenters and backyard boatbuilders is availability and price. As it was in the 1950s, plywood is still the cheapest boatbuilding material around, and it is ideal for boats that are uncomplicated in every way.

Although the objective is simplicity of construction, Bolger and Payson's Instant Boats can be radical creations. The Tortoise pram and Nymph dinghy are brilliantly simple boxes that still function as boats. The Nymph consists of five plywood panels that can be put together in eight hours. The dramatic Black Skimmer is a twenty-five-foot (7.6m) daysailer with an unstayed

yawl rig, twin leeboards, a clipper bow, camping-out accommodations in its little cabin, and the ability to float in less than a foot (30.4cm) of water. The eleven-foot-eight-inch (3.5m) Cartopper is an all-purpose vehicle for rowing, sailing, or small-outboard power. The famous Folding Schooner is perhaps the most adventurous Instant Boat—a thirty-one-foot by five-foot (9.4 by 1.5m) two-masted schooner with an open, sharpie hull, masts light enough to be carried by one person, and a design that permits the forward half of the boat to fold over the after half for handier trailering and storage. There are now thirty-six Instant Boats available in plans for home boatbuilders, and they are untraditional small craft by any measure.

Another Instant Boat is the eleven-foot-eight-inch (3.5m) Cartopper, a lightweight skiff for oar, outboard, or sail power, here being rowed on the coast of Maine.

Some new and untraditional designs are closer to small-boat traditions but equally creative in using new materials and carrying on the ever-lighter evolution of paddling boats and rowboats. A few examples are the lapstrake canoes that Tom Hill builds near Lake Champlain in Vermont and the light lapstrake rowboats and sailboats designed by England's Iain Oughtred and built by amateurs all over the world. Hill's canoes are influenced by the Rushton canoes of a hundred years ago—themselves marvels of strength and lightness—and are made from four-millimeter Bruynzeel marine plywood glued with

Above:

One of Tom Hill's ultralight canoes—this one a two-person design.

Left:

Phil Bolger's Black Skimmer, a shoal-draft overnight cruiser.

Tom Hill hefts the lightest of his creations—a nine-foot-six-inch (2.8m) canoe that weighs a mere twenty pounds (9.1kg). Hill designs and builds these canoes and provides plans for backyard boatbuilders.

epoxy in lapped stakes, and spruce gunwales to stiffen up the structure. Xynole cloth laid in epoxy strengthens the bottoms of these boats and protects them from abrasion. There are no ribs or frames inside these boats, and the eleven-foot-six-inch (3.5m) canoe weighs only twenty-seven pounds (12.2kg). It is also as lovely as an old Rushton. Tom Hill now builds five models of ultralight canoes from nine feet six inches (2.8m) to sixteen feet (4.8m)—the biggest one being a rowboat—and sells plans to home boatbuilders.

A similar exercise in glued-lapstrake construction is Iain Oughtred's Acorn dinghy, a Whitehall-type with plumb stem, graceful sheerline, and wineglass transom.

The Acorn is built on a simple frame of laminated members kept to a minimum, and the hull's real strength is the monocoque structure created by lapped-and-glued planks of eight-millimeter marine plywood. The eleven-foot-six-inch (3.5m) Acorn weighs one hundred pounds (45.4kg) with seats, floorboards, and transom of solid wood. In Oughtred's plan series for amateur builders, there are four sizes of Acorn dinghies, measuring from seven feet ten inches (2.3m) to fifteen feet (4.5m), and they are all perfect examples of a traditional rowboat/sailboat re-created with new materials. The Acorns are especially beautiful when finished bright inside so that all the mahogany glows, and painted in bold colors outside so that the shad-

ows of the lapped planking show the subtle curves of the hull. The Acorn dinghy is one of the most beautiful small boats in the world, traditional and untraditional at the same time.

Tom Hill's neighborhood up in Vermont is a nest of untraditional boatbuilders and designers. One of them is Steve Redmond. His Whisp rowing skiff is shown in the previous chapter because it is really more traditional than untraditional—a flatiron skiff that looks the part in all ways except for its poise, its modern delicacy of line and proportion. Redmond's Whisp is another ultralight boat, weighing seventy pounds (31.7kg) in the fifteen-and-a-half-foot (4.7m) version, seats and all, and yet another example of tradition meeting new thinking and materials.

North of Tom Hill and Steve Redmond on Lake Champlain is Ken Bassett of North Hero, Vermont, whose

Iain Oughtred's Acorn dinghy, a traditional lapstrake rowing boat reinterpreted in laminated wood and eight-millimeter marine plywood with almost no frame members. Its weight of a hundred pounds (45.4kg) is roughly one-third the weight of a similar boat of traditional construction.

One of the new generation of recreational rowing shells, Ken Bassett's Firefly is built in single and double versions with sliding seats and with spoon oars on outriggers.

Onion River Boat Works builds light, rakish recreational rowboats with sliding seats and outriggers. Bassett is another plywood experimenter. His boats are normally made from ¼-inch (6mm) marine plywood over strong but lean frames of spruce and yellow pine, with bronze screws, bronze ring nails, and epoxy for fastening. Bassett's twenty-two-foot (6.7m) Firefly, a boat for two rowers, weighs 140 pounds (63.5kg). Its eighteen-foot (5.4m) little sister, a single, weighs ninety pounds (40.8kg). Along with these untraditional rowing shells, Bassett builds a few traditional boats, including the lovely Liz, an eighteen-foot (5.4m) lapstrake pulling boat made from cedar planks on oak frames, as well as a mahogany outboard runabout that can be seen on page 118.

Two untraditional canoes for home-building, both extremely simple applications of lumberyard plywood, are Mike O'Brien's Six-Hour Canoe and Glen-L Marine's version of a Rob Roy canoe. The Rob Roy, named for and roughly based on the famous English cruising canoe of the 1860s, weighs only forty pounds (18.1kg) and is fourteen feet six inches (4.4m) long and twenty-nine inches (73.6cm) wide. It is made from two four-foot-by-eight-foot (1.2 by 2.4m) sheets of plywood, and its few pieces are stitched and glued together. Glen-

L, that legendary source for amateur boatbuilders, sells plans and patterns for the Rob Roy and many other small boats.

The Six-Hour Canoe, true to its name, can be constructed in one day with a long lunch hour from two sheets of ¼-inch (6mm) marine plywood and odds and ends of pine. It is a deceptively clever boat—dead-simple, lightweight, low-tech, low-risk, dory-looking with its angled ends and its flaring sides, unconventional, untraditional, and close to improbable. This fourteen-foot (4.2m) boat for amateur builders is a wonderful example of "Why didn't somebody think of this a long time ago?"

Dory-shaped and extremely simple in design and construction, the Six-Hour Canoe is made from ¼-inch (6mm) plywood and lumberyard pine. This fourteen-foot (4.3m) dory-canoe for a single paddler is intended for home construction.

Glen-L Marine's interpretation of the Rob Roy canoe is fourteen feet six inches (4.4m) long and weighs forty pounds (18.1kg). It is made from ¼-inch (6mm) plywood stitched and glued together, then sheathed with fiberglass.

Martin Marine's Appledore Pod
can be rigged for sail as well as for
rowing with an Oarmaster sliding-
seat and outrigger unit.

In the high-tech spectrum of untraditional small boats, there are some hulls molded from multiple thin veneers of wood that are able to take shapes impossible for lumberyard plywood to assume (although once the hulls are layered up they are essentially plywood), as well as boats made from—of all odd ingredients—wood and Dacron. The molded boats have a history at least as old as good waterproof glues (circa 1940). The category includes boats from the 1950s that are now fond memories, such as molded-plywood sailboats like the Thistle—all of its wood brightly varnished inside and out—as well as molded-plywood outboard runabouts that were equally lovely for their display of cedar or mahogany under multiple coats of varnish.

One of the most beautiful recreational rowboats in the world is the late Arthur Martin's sixteen-foot (4.8m) Appledore Pod, a slim double-ender made from cold-molded cedar and weighing seventy pounds (31.7kg). This is an epoxy-age rowing machine equipped with an Oarmaster sliding-seat unit, aluminum outriggers, and an optional sailing rig. During recent decades, the wood Appledore and its fiberglass cousins from Martin Marine

The handsome Pod is made from strips of cedar cold-molded to shape with epoxy and then given a tough epoxy finish that shows off the wood.

The eight-foot (2.4m) Westport dinghy from Monfort Associates shows off its intricate structure of thin wood framing braced with Kevlar cord. The covering here is clear Mylar rather than Dacron cloth. The boat weighs twenty-nine pounds (13.2kg).

in Kittery, Maine, have been important contributions to the popularity of rowing for exercise and sheer pleasure.

Of all the untraditional small boats that have come along in this century, none are more remarkable than the canoes and pulling boats invented and designed by Platt Monfort of Wiscasset, Maine. What Monfort calls Geodesic Airolite boats are made like the childrens' kayaks of old that had wood frames covered in canvas. But Monfort's boats, a legacy of his work with ultralight aircraft, are an elegant synthesis of thin, basketlike wood framing, Kevlar cord to brace the wood, and a covering of

Dacron cloth that shrinks drumhead-tight with the application of heat. There are more than twenty boats in Platt Monfort's catalog of plans and kits. This includes three small sailboats, eleven canoes, and Whitehall-style rowboats that measure from seven-and-a-half feet (2.2m) to fifteen feet (4.5m). The light weight of these boats is astonishing—twelve pounds (5.4kg) for the ten-and-a-half foot (3.2m) Snowshoe Lassie one-person canoe (the name is a tribute to J. Henry Rushton's legendary Wee Lassie canoe) and from sixty-five to seventy pounds (29.5 to 31.7kg) for the fifteen-foot (4.5m) Whitehall type.

Perhaps equally astonishing is the way that they look like real boats rather than boat-shaped airplane wings.

As it has been for the last hundred years, new materials and new applications of familiar materials are a certainty for the twenty-first century. What new boats these new directions will make possible is good food for thought—the kind of thinking that brought us the untraditional small boats we see here. Somewhere, someone is already thinking such thoughts and experimenting in the workshop and on the water.

Note: Sources for plans, patterns, kits, and completed boats are given in an appendix at the back of the book.

Left, top:

An eleven-foot-five-inch (3.5m) Nimrod canoe that weighs only fourteen pounds (6.4kg).

Left, bottom:

One of Monfort's sixteen-foot (4.9m) Snow Shoe canoes fitted with a sliding seat for fast rowing. This canoe weighs thirty-two pounds (14.5kg).

CHAPTER 5

Classic Sailing Yachts

Sailing around in yachts for amusement or self-aggrandizement can be traced at least as far back as the ancient Egyptians. Their cruises were described by the Roman poet Horace as typically Eastern luxury and foolishness: "They change their sky and not their soul, who run across the sea. We work hard at doing nothing—we seek happiness in yachts." Nevertheless, there is and always has been happiness in yachts. Even the Romans fell under their spell. There is nothing like being on the water, and nothing like the peculiar pleasure and responsibility of your own little island.

You can hide out in it, travel around in it, share it with your friends, show off on it, keep it gleaming as an announcement of your skills or your taste or your money, and use it in so many ways as an extension of your ego.

Yachts and even small boats are extensions of their owners' egos—and expressions of their values. After the Greeks, Egyptians, and Romans sought happiness in yachts, the Vikings enjoyed them in the same way more than a thousand years later. The exquisite Oseberg ship, dug up in Norway

in 1904, is thought to have been a royal vessel for Queen Asa, who was buried in it around 850 A.D. In the meantime, all over the world, important people whose realms included waterways and coasts enjoyed vessels not built or intended for work, as many of the important people themselves were not. Yachts are unserious little ships—although they can be the most serious vessels in the world when commanded by the Grand Vizier, the Emperor's tax collector along a hundred miles (161km) of coastline, or maybe even by you.

Most yachts from the dim past can be identified as small, fancy vessels used for official or ceremonial service. Boats of this type can be found in the histories of China, Japan, the Middle East, and Europe. Modern yachting, and the word itself, began with the Dutch of the 1600s who traded with a suddenly enlarged world from their damp little fringe of Europe. The Dutch used *jachts* for official business and pleasure in their harbors, *zees*, and canals. They made these boats such fancy, handy, and desirable vessels that

the English, alternately at war or in league with the Dutch in the seventeenth century, took notice. Charles II was given a fifty-two-foot (15.8m) Dutch *jacht schip* in 1660, and a year later both he and his brother James had new English-built yachts for racing and carrying parties of revelers on cruises.

Seeking happiness in yachts may not have needed a royal example to take hold in the Europe and America of

the past four hundred years, but royal example—from the kings of England and Scandinavia to Kaiser Wilhelm of Germany and Alfonso XIII of Spain in the twentieth century—established yachting's prestige. Yachting became a sport—a skilled leisure activity—that had cachet. And the two branches of the activity, cruising and racing, developed different yachts and different devotees. The sailing yachts in this chapter represent variations on those two themes, and they are all yachts of the twentieth century. Only a few nineteenth-century yachts survive anywhere in the world.

A discussion of classic sailing yachts could not have a better beginning than *Ticonderoga*, launched in 1936 for one of the Brahmins of Boston as an elegant, clipper-style cruising yacht that her designer thought might have some racing potential. She certainly did. During the great post-war years of ocean racing, *Ticonderoga* was often at the front of the fleet, and competed in nearly all the major races on both coasts of America and in the Caribbean. She was designed to the seventy-three-foot (22.2m) maximum length of the racing rules, always had good crew and good management, and set many a course record. Her most renowned feat of record-setting was a first-overall finish in the 1965 TransPacific Race, averaging more than ten knots for the 2,400-mile (3,480km) slide from Los Angeles to Honolulu. L. Francis Herreshoff designed *Ticonderoga* to be as lovely as she was fast—and to be a throwback to the nineteenth century. At a time when big ocean-racing yachts were modeled after fishing schooners, tough and plain and earnest, this yacht had the aesthetics of the 1851 schooner yacht *America*—clipper bow with bowsprit/pulpit, trailboards carved with leaves, a golden eagle on the transom, and carved dolphins at the break in her sheerline. Big *Ti* is one of the most admired classic sailing yachts in the world.

Opposite, left:

The view down big Ti's teak decks as she booms along in a brisk wind.

Opposite, right:

Gilded dolphins decorate Ticonderoga's sheerline.

Above:

Ticonderoga's dining saloon now welcomes Caribbean charter guests.

A fleet of Concordia yawls cruises the Maine coast. There were 103 Concordias built, and all of them are still in one piece. Most remain in commission and are well kept by their owners.

Another variation on the racing boat that can cruise or the cruising boat that can race, and one totally different from the mass and style of *Ticonderoga*, is a yacht designed by C. Raymond Hunt, another yacht-design genius. The Concordia yawls were designed by Hunt in thirty-nine-foot (11.8m) and forty-one-foot (12.4m) versions and built by the renowned German yacht yard of Abeking and Rassmussen. They took advantage of a post-war downsizing of the yachting fleet here and in Europe,

and also provided American yachtsmen with a first-quality racing or cruising vehicle at a bargain price. The Concordias were off-the-shelf rather than custom-built, and in Germany after World War II their builders were eager for the work and for the dollars. There were 103 Concordias launched throughout the 1950s and early 1960s, and it is a tribute to their construction that every one of them is still around. Their racing record includes two Bermuda Race victories and a clean sweep by Ray

Hunt and his family in six out of six races during Britain's Cowes Week in 1955.

Yet another racing and cruising classic is *Stormy Weather*, a powerful fifty-four-foot (16.4m) yawl designed by Olin Stephens for his brother Rod, who campaigned her in nearly every race on the East Coast and Great Lakes from the season of her launching in 1934 to the 1970s. *Stormy Weather* is a superb example of the Sparkman and Stephens style of conservative lines, meticulous engineering of rig and systems by Rod Stephens, and the ability of Olin Stephens to blend art

Above:

Concordias were all but perfectly constructed and finished by the craftsmen of Germany's Abeking and Rassmussen yacht yard.

Left:

The European pine paneling provides a warm touch down below.

Amorita, *one of the surviving New York 30s built in 1905 for members of the New York Yacht Club, shows off her fine lines and big gaff-rigged sailplan.*

and science into a vessel that does everything a sailing classic should do: look wonderful, cruise safely and comfortably, and win races.

Older cruising/racing classics are the New York 30s and Buzzards Bay 25s, both intended as fleets of identical yachts able to compete evenly without fussy handicapping formulas. Eighteen New York 30s were built in 1905 for members of the New York Yacht Club. Only four of the Buzzards Bay 25s were built in 1914; they were as expensive as they were beautiful. Both were designed by

Nathanael Herreshoff, then at the top of his form as the world's principal creator of racing yachts. Both also have an Edwardian elegance: varnished-wood house structures, big gaff sailplans, long tapering ends, and what now seem to be perfect proportions from a time when designers and owners valued the aesthetic impact of these expensive playthings.

Sailing yachts used strictly for racing include the "Meter" boats spawned in 1906 by Europe's International Rule, a formula for yacht designers and

An Edwardian-era yacht, Amorita has long tapering ends and details that seem delicate by today's huskier standards. Her overall length is forty-three feet six inches (13.3m); her waterline length is approximately thirty feet (9.1m)

Right and far right:

Before World War II, one-design racing sailboats like these were all made of wood. Today most of the hundreds of classes of one-design boats in the world are made of fiberglass.

builders that was intended to encourage solid, safe, exciting racing in boats of reasonably similar dimensions and potential. The most famous of these classes is the Twelve-Meter fleet that challenged and defended the America's Cup from 1956 to 1987. The most active of these classes is a Six-Meter fleet, which competes in Europe and America in custom-built boats that are beautiful and somewhat experimental. A "development" class of one-design boats, the Sixes are designed and constructed to a rule that is deliberately broad rather than rigid in order to encourage innovation. For most of this century, Six-Meter sloops have attracted owners and racers wealthy enough and creative enough

An elite wooden boat custom-designed and custom-built for racing is this Six Meter sloop.

to campaign adventurous new boats. Even in this age of plastics, wood is often the material chosen to build them. Wood is selected for its sheer suitability in an exercise of craftsmanship, creativity, and—yes—plastic characteristics when the wood is hot-molded or cold-molded into a boat.

Cruising yachts have as many variations as their racing sisters—and as many varieties of owners and adventures. A sailboat designed and built for cruising can take a family of sailors around the world. At any given time in recent decades, there have been hundreds of single-handed adventurers, couples, and entire families on the world's oceans making long voyages that only a few power yachts can safely manage.

Before Joshua Slocum, a retired master of big sailing ships, cruised alone around the world in an old Cape Cod yawl built for oystering, and then wrote a book about it, few small yachts crossed the broad oceans. In the nineteenth century such feats were considered foolhardy and dangerous even for professionals like Slocum. But soon enough amateur sailors began to make long cruises out of sight of land. By the 1920s, the type of yacht thought suitable for these adventures was a double-ended sloop or ketch modeled after the famous rescue vessels of Norway, which were brawny double-enders designed by a Scottish-Norwegian, Colin Archer, to go offshore in any weather.

Direction, shown here, is a prime example of the type: deep-keeled, heavily built and rigged, deliberately slow and predictable, tight and comfortable below, and able to ride the sea like a buoy. *Direction* was built in 1929 for a young man to sail from New York to Greenland with a crew of friends, which the boat did, although she was disabled on the Greenland coast and nearly didn't make it back. From 1946 to the 1980s she was owned by Carl and Margaret Vilas. They sailed nearly every season from Long Island Sound to Nova Scotia and back, even when they were both in their mid-seventies.

A more compact interpretation of the deep and husky boat for ocean cruising is *Annie*, a small, gaff-rigged yawl designed in 1932 by Fenwick Williams and built in 1980 by Maine's Arundel Shipyard. Like many a small

cruising yacht, she has fishing-boat ancestry, but no fishing boat ever behaved as nimbly or looked as pretty as this miniature of her larger working and yachting sisters. *Annie* is only twenty-four feet (7.3m) across her teak deck, but she looks much larger.

Another classic pocket cruiser, this one a shallower and even smaller boat fitted with a centerboard, is *Martha*. She was designed in 1953 by S.S. Crocker and built in 1967 by Joel White. The clipper-ship aesthetics that are seen on a larger scale and with greater fanciness in *Ticonderoga* can be seen in *Martha*, with her clipper bow, dolphin-carved trailboards, and elliptical transom. The small fishing sloops of the nineteenth century in Maine

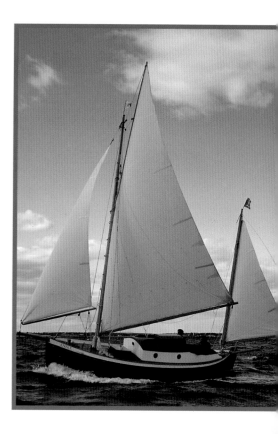

T wo heavy, beamy, solidly built cruising boats—the twenty-four-foot (7.3m) Annie (above) and the thirty-three-foot (10.1m) Direction (left).

Below: The replica Crosby catboat Breck Marshall *under sail near Mystic Seaport. Developed for fishing in southern New England, the catboat is roomy, stable, and distinctive as a recreational boat.*

Opposite: Francis Herreshoff's celebrated Rozinante.

copied features of clippers in the same way, and this little coastal cruiser is reminiscent of the Friendship sloops. *Martha* is only nineteen feet nine inches (6m) on deck.

Cruising sailboats are often yacht versions of small fishing boats, and one of the great classics in this tradition is the Cape Cod catboat. *Breck Marshall* was built by Barry Thomas in Mystic Seaport Museum's small-boat shop in 1987, and she sails the Mystic River every sum-

mer with Seaport visitors aboard. The *Marshall* is a yacht version of the fishing and oystering catboats of Cape Cod that evolved in the last half of the nineteenth century. Catboats are broad, relatively shallow boats with big centerboards, "barn-door" rudders, and single large gaff-rigged sails. This plain but handsome little boat is a near-exact replica of a catboat launched by the famous Crosby boatyard of Osterville, Massachusetts, around 1900.

L. Francis Herreshoff was a yacht-design genius who reinterpreted themes and types from the yachting past with such originality that the results were entirely new creations. One of the L.F.H. classics is a twenty-eight-foot (8.5m) canoe yawl he named *Rozinante*, after Don Quixote's old horse. Canoe yawls were canoe-form pocket cruisers popular with coastal voyagers in England in the 1890s. They were called yawls not for their rigs, but for their similarity in size and service to the yawl boats carried on big ships. *Rozinante*, canoelike and delicate, and with Francis Herreshoff's characteristic Chesapeake-Bay sailplan, has all but perfect curves and proportions. By all accounts, she's a wonderful coastal cruising boat with speed, agility, and no bad habits.

Two similar exercises in reinterpreting the past and coming up with totally original results are *Mist* and *Toadstool*, a cat-ketch and a miniature schooner-yacht designed by Canada's William Garden. It can safely be said that there is no designer of yachts or small boats in the world who brings more art to the exercise, and these two examples of Garden's work are proof. Cat-ketches—two masts, the taller one forward in the eyes of the boat, and both with single sails—were used in a variety of fisheries up and down the Atlantic coast in the nineteenth century. They were simple open boats for alongshore and harbor use. *Mist* is a full-bodied coastal cruising yacht with something of the hull lines of a ship's boat, a long house structure, and beautiful sweeps of line from plumb bow to elliptical transom. She is one of Bill Garden's

Mist *(left) and* Toadstool *(right) show Bill Garden's artistry in designing small yachts. The artistry extends below decks, too. Above, we see Mist's cozy accommodations.*

handsomest creations. One of Garden's most whimsical creations is *Toadstool*, a boat he designed for his own use. She is a toy cruising schooner with an exaggerated clipper bow, a deep curve of sheerline, and house lines that continue aft to form a cockpit coaming and then a davit for the dinghy. Down below are a varnished-wood galley and a main cabin, its cozy quarters warmed by a tiny black-iron cookstove.

Schooners have always been favored cruising yachts, and *Mary Harrigan* and *Half Moon* are just two of many such classic models. The first is a big workboat-style schooner with dramatic tanbark sails, and the second is one of the yachts John Alden shaped with inspiration from the great North Atlantic fishing schooners. *Mary Harrigan* is fifty feet (15.2m) long with a twelve-foot (3.6m) beam and a five-foot (1.5m) draft. She was built to a 1924 Nathanael Herreshoff design that was inspired by one of New England's nineteenth-century pilot schooners. She's a big, handsome, clipper-style schooner of twenty-six tons (23.4t), an ocean voyager that spends most of her year in the Caribbean on charter.

Half Moon, shown here, is forty-three feet by eleven

feet six inches by six feet four inches (13.1 by 3.5 by 2m). She is smaller and finer-lined than *Mary Harrigan*, and is a classic John Alden yacht that has enjoyed meticulous care from a succession of owners over seven decades. *Half Moon* has almost always looked as perfect as she does here, with flawless paintwork, plate-glass varnish, and a high polish on her brass.

"We seek happiness in yachts," said the Egyptians to Horace's Muse. In these few examples of sailing clas-sics, it is not difficult to see why. They are vehicles for racing, for poking around the coast with a few friends, and for communing with Mother Nature in the form of wind in the sails and water burbling away under the counter. They are an ancient source of happiness for their designers, builders, owners, crews, and even us spectators.

Note: Sources for plans, patterns, kits, and completed boats

Half Moon, *a classic small John Alden schooner.*

CHAPTER 6

Classic Power Yachts

Some of the earliest applications of steam power at the end of the eighteenth century and of gasoline power near the end of the nineteenth century were in boats, and the power yacht evolved as a distinct type by the 1820s. But yachtsmen were rowers and sailors then, and the newfangled technology of steam was not readily accepted on the water. Engines were noisy, smelly, sooty, fussy, and threatening to the venerable conceits of commerce under sail—a commerce in which many yachtsmen, then and since, made their fortunes. In 1827, England's Royal Yacht Squadron decreed that "any member applying a steam engine to his yacht shall be disqualified thereby and cease to be a member." This rule was rescinded sixteen years later when Queen Victoria and Prince Albert acquired a steam yacht. Where the Queen led, others had to follow, or at least not stand in the way. Nevertheless, the prejudices of sailors, rowers, and paddlers persist. Today's sailors disdain "stinkpotters," and the Adirondack Museum hosts a rowing, paddling, sailing No-Octane Regatta every June.

The first classic power yachts were steam yachts, which were generally built of iron or steel and given long, slim hulls that looked like clipper ships shorn of their masts. The early power yachts had clipper bows and bowsprits, nice curves of sheerline, rounded and tucked-in sterns, and varnished-wood deckhouses and deck furniture. They were handsome, impressive vessels. Gilded Age New Yorkers favored such power yachts, and by the season of 1900 they equaled the number of sailing yachts in the New York Yacht Club fleet. Meanwhile, small steam launches fulfilled the power-yachting dreams of people in the middle class. The steam launches were elegant little machines that featured fantail sterns, plumb stems, varnished decks and interior woodwork, wicker chairs, and awning-striped canvas tops. Their machinery looks crude to us now and their slim hulls seem quaint, but the steam launches of a hundred years ago were sophisticated packages. As one latter-day steam expert has testified: "Recreational steam vessels enjoyed only a few years

Relatively few steam launches have survived from the 1890s, and most of them are in museums. This one is a replica from the Pat Spurlock's Elliott Bay Steam Launch Co.

of increasing popularity and refinement in the 1880s and 1890s; but a century of steamship experience was reflected in their design."

The simple gasoline engines that came along in the 1890s quickly eclipsed naphtha engines and electric motors in boats, and they replaced steam for a reason that was more legal than mechanical. Steam was doomed in the United States by a federal law that required anyone who operated a steam engine to have a steam engineer's license. A robber baron could afford to hire an engineer

for his one-hundred-foot (30.4m) steam yacht; but an ordinary summer cottager had to get his own license or, better yet, get a boat with a gas engine. Gasoline engines were so popular by the turn of the century that nearly half the boats reported under construction in the United States by *Rudder* magazine for the 1901 boating season had gas power. There were hundreds of small shops all over the United States and Canada building one-cylinder and two-cylinder engines for boats, farms, factories, and even a few automobiles.

The steam-launch replica and the Herreshoff gasoline launch shown in these pages are similar vehicles, designed long and slim to get the most from moderate power, although the gas-engine launch is larger. Its twenty-eight-horsepower engine also takes up less space than the steam apparatus, its attendant boiler, and a supply of coal or wood. Launches like the Herreshoff twenty-six footer (8m) were favored as tenders for larger yachts and for yacht-club service. The twenty-six-foot (8m) Herreshoff launch in the photos was a tender for the America's Cup defender *Resolute* in her successful contest with Sir Thomas Lipton's fourth *Shamrock* in the summer of 1920. Later she served Long Island's Seawanhaka Corinthian Yacht Club as a launch to ferry members and guests to and

from yachts at anchor. These days she spends her summers taking Mystic Seaport Museum visitors for joyrides on the Mystic River.

Gas-powered cruisers did not come along until engines were powerful enough to push larger hulls full of accommodations for overnight trips, although this happened very quickly. Before World War I, custom-built cruisers with gasoline power began to appear. Many of them looked like the turn-of-the-century launches with the addition of a small cabin forward, a helm station with no windshield amidships, and an after cockpit that often had a shelter top. This configuration persists in small overnight cruisers today. Bigger cruisers—including commuters, those express boats that took men and women to

Mystic Seaport Museum's *Captain Ted Kay, appropriately costumed, drives the twenty-six-foot (8m) Herreshoff gasoline launch that once served the 1920 America's Cup defender* Resolute.

A *Fay and Bowen Junior Runabout from the 1920s cruises Lake Placid. This twenty-five-foot (7.6m) sport boat, with its long forward deck and rear cockpit with wicker chairs, was the final refinement of the gasoline launch.*

work—came along in quantity after World War I, along with mass-produced boats and the beginnings of the boating industry as we know it today.

The Great War accelerated an engine technology that was already moving quickly before 1917, and after America's nineteen months of war a huge surplus of engines for trucks, tanks, and aircraft came on the market at bargain prices. A lot of the roar of the Roaring Twenties was supplied by these engines in workboats, speedboats, rumrunners, launches, and cruisers. In the 1920s, the power yacht came into its own. There were mass-produced launches and cruisers from Matthews, Luders, Elco, Fay and Bowen, and many others. There were rakish, custom-built commuters that sped the mil-

lionaires who lived in big waterfront cities like New York and Detroit to work at fifty miles per hour (80kph). There were diesel yachts more than a hundred feet long (30.4m) that had all the baronial trappings of the previous generation's steam yachts, including marble fireplaces in their saloons and skeet-shooting facilities on their afterdecks.

We show a few typical classics from the 1920s and early 1930s in these pages. The Fay and Bowen Junior Runabout was the final evolution of the versatile but (by the 1920s) relatively slow-speed gasoline launch. It was an elegant boat with its brass fittings, long forward deck that sheltered an inadequate engine, and roomy cockpit with wicker chairs. But it failed to qualify as a speedboat in the sudden surge of fast-boat customers that came along in the 1920s and made the fortunes of builders like Chris-Craft and Gar Wood. Although they are collector's items today, Fay and Bowen boats were considered slow and old-fashioned in the Jazz Age.

Typical early cruisers and motor yachts are *Tenango*, *Lawana*, *Tradition*, and *Principia*, shown here. The oldest is *Lawana*, an early raised-deck cruiser that was built in 1911 by Taylor and Grandy in Burton, Washington. This roomy and comfortable forty-foot (12.1m) vessel is characteristic of the cruisers and the sportfishing boats that were built by the thousands before 1930 and were given the boxy good looks of 1920s sedans and limousines. Uncharacteristic is *Lawana*'s full-to-the-stern deckhouse with glass windshield and windows, a concession to Pacific Northwest wind and weather. Also uncharacteris-

tic is how great she looks for a wooden boat nearly a hundred years old. Boats built in the abundantly wooded Northwest had the best of materials and craftsmanship, as well as caring owners and yards skilled in maintaining boats. Very few raised-deck cruisers from the 1920s survive elsewhere.

Two mass-produced power classics from the 1920s and early 1930s are *Tenango* and *Tradition*. Elco had been mass-producing cruisers and small motor yachts for fifteen years by the time the forty-two-foot (12.8m) *Tenango* was built in 1930, and a certain perfection was achieved by designer Glen Tremaine and the Elco craftsmen. Elco "flat-tops" like this one are now very desirable classics because of their good looks, good behavior, and sheer utility as cruising vehicles. The proportions of this

A very early raised-deck cruiser with gasoline power, Lawana leads a parade of vintage powerboats at the Classic Boat Festival in Victoria, British Columbia, Canada.

forty-two-footer (12.8m) are just about perfect, and the quantity of varnished wood with painted surfaces for contrast seems to be equally ideal.

Tradition was built by Chris-Craft in 1929 as one of the earliest of sixty-five nearly identical thirty-eight-foot (11.5m) commuter yachts that were launched from 1928 to 1931, during the peak of the glamorous phenomenon of commuting to work by boat. Chris-Craft's speedboat heritage can be seen in the varnished-mahogany, runabout-style hull; commuter features are a forward cockpit with steering wheel and engine controls for the nautical

Right:
T*he gleaming helm station of the forty-two foot (12.8m) Elco Motor yacht* Tenango.

Below:
A*nother boat parade, this one in Seattle, is led by a classic big Elco.*

A big speedboat with a control station behind its forward windshield, a day cabin with galley amidships, and a cockpit aft, the Chris-Craft thirty-eight-foot (11.5m) commuter was designed to deliver executives from waterfront homes to city offices. This one, restored by Mike and Anne Matheson, is Tradition.

chauffeur, and a two-hundred-horsepower V8 engine that delivers speeds of up to thirty miles per hour (48kph). This is a real marine limousine, built to flash into town from the owner's waterfront home and then be tied up for the workday at the docks of a city yacht club.

A rare big motor yacht built in wood is the ninety-six-foot (29.2m) *Principia,* a 1928 product of Seattle's renowned Lake Union Drydock. This is a classic design by Ted Geary with a fantail stern, a plumb stem, a workboat-style pilothouse and deck structures, and two masts whose functions are largely theatrical. *Principia* is owned by Philadelphia's Independence Seaport, formerly the Philadelphia Maritime Museum, which bought her in deteriorated condition and gave her a flawless restoration. She now serves charter parties and guests of the Museum, cruising in Florida during the winter and in

Philadelphia and points north during the summer. The fact that *Principia* and three of her near-sister ships are still around is a tribute to Lake Union's workmanship.

Another classic wooden motor yacht, the "Florida houseboat," has survived in some numbers for more than eighty years after the first one was launched in 1910 by the Mathis Yacht Building Company of Camden, New Jersey. As many as a dozen of these boats survive, including several in Florida, where they were once fixtures on Indian Creek in Miami Beach. Designed by John Trumpy, with shallow draft for negotiating the Intracoastal Waterway on trips to and from the Sunshine State, these wide, full-bodied diesel yachts are shaped more for capacity than beauty. Nevertheless, in the 1920s and the 1930s, they were built for families with names like Firestone and DuPont, and the surviving examples are much admired at

Principia, one of the great luxury yachts built in the 1920s by Lake Union Drydock in Seattle, during her restoration at Billings Diesel and Marine in Stonington, Maine.

antique boat shows and rallies. The most familiar Mathis-Trumpy "houseboat" is the former presidential yacht *Sequoia*, which was built in 1925 for Philadelphia banker Richard Cadwalader.

The Depression delivered a near-fatal blow to the powerboat industry, especially at the luxury end of the market. Boatbuilders survived on smaller and/or cheaper products, and many of the dazzling commuters and motor yachts of the Jazz Age ended up for sale at bargain prices in the early 1930s. But at the New York Boat Show in

January 1929, almost ten months before the stock market crashed, a flamboyant Floridian introduced a then-low-priced motor yacht that would become a classic. Frank Pembroke Huckins designed and built his yachts to be extremely lightweight for their size, with thin mahogany planking over an oak framework, and with many laminated pieces. The Huckins yachts were light, strong, fast boats that were built in a variety of models, all with a stark patrol-boat style that had the no-nonsense attractiveness we see on the road today in Jeeps and Land Rovers. A surviving Huckins yacht is not a rarity. Indeed, of the 430 Huckins yachts built in wood at the company's boatyard on the Ortega River in Jacksonville, Florida, around three hundred are thought to still be intact.

During the 1930s, Huckins built boats for sport-fishing as well as motor yachts, as did such builders of family cruisers as Matthews, Elco, Chris-Craft, and Wheeler, which built Ernest Hemingway's famous *Pilar* for marlin fishing off Havana. Fishing in the ocean for everything from bluefish to giant tuna was a

new sport in the 1930s and 1940s, and boats were modified rather than built for the angling adventures of yachtsmen and charter skippers. The classic sport-fishing boat, with its sweeping raised deck, its low cockpit with fishing chairs aft, and its helm station on a flying bridge above the action, was virtually invent-ed by the Rybovich family in their boatyard in West Palm Beach. Ever since the first one was launched in 1947, Rybovich sportfishing boats have been the clas-sics of the sport.

One of the most popular diesel yachts of the 1920s and 1930s was the Mathis-Trumpy "Florida house-boat," intended for summer cruises in the North and winter sojourns in Florida. This is the eighty-five-foot (26m) Enticer, *built in 1935.*

Up in Maine during the 1930s, another distinctive powerboat type was evolving as a yachtsman's version of the tough, able, and nimble Down East lobsterboat. "Summer boats" and "picnic boats" have been a tradition on the Maine coast for seventy years, and the most stylish were built by the Cranberry Isles firm of Bunker and Ellis. A classic Bunker and Ellis product is the forty-two-foot (12.8m) *Jericho*, built in 1956 with a graceful blend of lobsterboat hull curves and a deckhouse and helm station in varnished Honduras mahogany. Nearly all lobsterboats are beautiful, but connoisseurs consider *Jericho* to be the prettiest boat of her type on the coast of Maine.

Considered the prettiest lobster-yacht on the coast of Maine, Jericho is a leisure-class version of her working sisters in the Maine-coast lobsterboat fleet.

Another Maine-built classic is *Black Knight*, which was launched in 1968 as *Cassiar* by Goudy and Stevens of East Boothbay. The husky eighty-two-foot (25m) *Black Knight* was designed by Walter McInnis as an offshore cruising and sportfishing yacht. She was shown off to the world in the America's Cup contests at Newport in the 1970s and 1980s, when she was the vehicle for the New York Yacht Club's Race Committee. With her exalted- workboat style, a Walter McInnis specialty, she has been described by one expert as representing "a standard of perfection in the design of modern displacement powerboats that has rarely been equaled."

A motor yacht with working-boat huskiness and handsomeness, along with the flawless finish of a luxury yacht, Black Knight is shown here on station during an America's Cup summer in Newport, Rhode Island, with the New York Yacht Club's Race Committee on board.

Power yachts that are inspired by, reminiscent of, or finished off as deluxe versions of working boats are an old tradition on the power side of the yachting divide. This is matched on the sail side by yachts descended from local fishing types, schooners reminiscent of South Seas or Caribbean trading vessels, and sailboats of all kinds with clipper-ship trimmings. Certainly the most familiar fleets of workboat-style power yachts are the Grand Banks diesel cruisers in all their varieties and sizes, as well as the boats launched by their imitators. Originally built of teak in Hong Kong, the Grand Banks boats are now constructed of fiberglass. They are not copies of anything, and are a brilliant synthesis of husky fishboat/yardboat hulls and boxy deckhouses and pilothouses that look just right and contain all the comforts of a floating home.

A smaller version of the same kind of brilliance is John Atkin's design for a twenty-two-foot (6.7m) boat he calls Ninigret for the Rhode Island locale where the original boat spends her summers. John Atkin and his father, William, have been masters of adapting, reinterpreting, and, perhaps more than anything, understanding workboat and yacht traditions from all over the world. This boat is a light little plywood skiff for casting after bass and bluefish in Block Island Sound. Power is an outboard motor in a well, the cabin top is a removable piece of canvas supported by ash battens, and in the little cabin are two seat berths and a water closet. Ninigret is the sort of boat that a yachtsman might have created from a working hull in the 1930s, but John Atkin has given the exercise the lines and proportions of a little yacht. This is a boat designed for home-building, and plans are available from Atkin and Company in Noroton, Connecticut. Finished Ninigrets are available from Freedom Boatworks of Baraboo, Wisconsin.

John Atkin's Ninigret design is a handy, handsome, workboat-style launch with moderate outboard power and two seat berths in its little cabin.

Fiberglass cruisers replaced wood cruisers very quickly during the 1960s, but the postwar world produced its share of classic power yachts in wood. We consider two of them here. The first is a Lyman wood-lapstrake sea skiff, the second a Chris-Craft cruiser from the 1950s. The Lymans were built on Lake Erie to a basic Jersey skiff design that was perfect for family outings, fishing trips on bays and lakes, and even overnight cruising aboard the bigger Lymans. They were wood-lapstrake products of the 1950s—practical, plain of line, relatively inexpensive, and given a quantity of nice varnished-mahogany details,

from big workboat-style windshields to broad expanses of bright wood on their transoms. A number of builders produced "sea skiffs" like them from 1945 to 1965, but the Lymans are the classics.

The Chris-Craft cruisers of the 1950s were a lot like the Cadillacs their owners drove to the boatyard—big, flashy, curvilinear, and decorated with chrome trim. They were all classics of their type, but the mid-1950s Chris-Craft Corvettes and Constellations stand out as especially well-proportioned and aesthetically pleasing artifacts from that decade of prosperity, conformity, and attractive vulgarity.

What we have in these postwar cruisers are boats that represent fulfilled dreams of getting out on the water in style, comfort, and safety. These are boats in which to pursue fish, to run all the way down the bay and anchor off that beach—the one we found last year—for an afternoon of swimming, to take us away for a long-weekend cruise to nowhere in particular, or to let us leave the cold north and cruise southward through the interesting Intracoastal to live all winter aboard our own floating house in Florida.

Note: Sources for plans, patterns, kits, and completed boats are given in an appendix at the back of the book.

▸ *Top left:*

A *mahogany-and-metal detail from a 1950s Chris-Craft cruiser.*

▸ *Left:*

W*ood-lapstrake sea skiffs like this one were built all over the U.S. between roughly 1945 and 1965. Of all the sea skiffs from small and large builders, Lyman products like this one are considered the classics.*

CHAPTER 7

Classic Speedboats

Speed came to boats less than a decade after the German patents on the internal-combustion engine ran out in 1895. With no licensing complications, and with the principles of Dr. Otto's "explosive" engine understood, blacksmiths, machinists, trained engineers, and amateur motorheads began to experiment with gasoline engines all over the world. A boat was one of the simplest vehicles in which to test and use these fascinating contraptions that were fated to change everything—at first the long, slim, canoe-form hulls of the existing steam and naphtha launches, and finally light, flat-bottomed "planing hulls" that could climb up over their own waves and skim across the water.

By 1904, the Herreshoff brothers in Rhode Island had built and raced a forty-five-foot (13.7m) displacement boat with a seventy-five-horsepower Mercedes engine at a speed of 26.29 miles per hour (42kph). In 1907, Clinton Crane's *Dixie II*, another long and slim displacement racing boat, cracked thirty miles per hour (48kph). In 1910, both a small French

"hydroplane" and a huge English racing boat with 760 horsepower shot across the water at more than forty miles per hour (64kph). During the next year, boats in the United States and Europe did better than fifty miles per hour (80kph), and during 1912–1913 boats on both sides of the Atlantic hit a mile (1.6km) a minute. By 1920, Gar Wood in his first *Miss America* had set a world water speed record of 77.89 miles per hour (124.6kph).

The boats, engines, and men making these remarkable strides in speed, engineering, boatbuilding, and sheer daring were poised at the beginning of the 1920s to create something new: the speedboat—a civilized, civilian version of the racing machines. The mahogany bullet with comfortable leather seats and a windshield was developed in Detroit around 1918 by the great raceboat designer John Hacker. In the roaring decade ahead, it would be copied by speedboat builders all over North America and Europe. The mahogany runabout appeared just as warehouses were full to the rafters with surplus machinery from World War I: ninety-horsepower Curtiss OX-5 engines built for Jenny biplanes, two-hundred-horsepower Hispano-Suizas, and mighty twelve-cylinder Liberty engines that could be tweaked up to as much as five hundred horsepower.

The C.C. Smith and Sons boat shop of Algonac, Michigan, combined their own version of John Hacker's successful twenty-six-foot (7.9m) two-cockpit runabout with a ninety-horsepower Curtiss surplus engine, and shipped three examples east for the 1922 New York Motorboat Show. On the mahogany flanks of these boats was a new name for both the company and the boat—Chris-Craft. The Smith family pioneered not only speedboats, but the business of building and selling them. They set up an assembly-line system, used Philippine mahogany rather than the more expensive Honduras mahogany, bought the OX-5 engines for as little as $50 each when ordered by the carload, established a network of loyal dealers across the United States, and, more than anything else, delivered a boat the public not only wanted but could afford. Chris-Craft sales grew from $53,825 in 1922 to $3,254,923 in 1929.

A look at the 1920s Chris-Craft runabouts in these pages will go far toward explaining their success. The Jazz Age Chris-Crafts, with their upswept decks, square open-

Page 100:
The replica of Miss Daytona, *a 151 Class racing boat from the 1920s, picks up speed.*

Page 101:
Chris-Craft speedboats from the 1950s.

Right, top:
A detail of the Chris-Craft logo.

Right, bottom:
The original twenty-six-foot (7.9m) Chris-Craft runabout from the 1920s in all her varnished-mahogany glory.

During the 1940s and 1950s, mahogany runabouts acquired more curves and more chrome trim—an automobile influence that produced some lovely boats.

ing windshields, and chrome trim, had all the style of Pierce-Arrow touring cars. Their competitors, including John Hacker's more expensive HackerCraft Dolphin runabouts, enjoyed equal success through the 1920s, as did boats from custom builders like Hutchinson Boat Works in the Thousand Islands and Canada's Ditchburn and Minett-Shields enterprises.

The speeds of boats racing for the American Power Boat Association's Gold Cup had been accelerating each year since 1904, and the 1920 and 1921 contests were dominated by Gar Wood—millionaire, sportsman, boatbuilder, egotist, and daredevil. Wood's mighty *Miss America* racing boats, which were powered by multiple Liberty aircraft engines, were exercises in putting the most horsepower in the least boat. By 1921, Gold Cup speeds had crept to over seventy miles per hour (112kph), and costs to compete had grown to the breaking point of nearly all budgets except Gar Wood's. For the 1922 Gold Cup, a change in the rules specified hulls of twenty-five feet (7.6m) or more and single engines of 625 cubic inches or less. The new rules meant that this would now be a race among gentlemen in "gentlemen's runabouts." The new rules inhibited wild speeds and brute-force boats, but for more than a decade they encouraged the creation of some of the greatest speedboats the world has ever seen.

A nautical touring car from the 1920s, Javelin *is a Fay and Bowen Runabout 27 built in the winter of 1925–1926 for the chef of the Saranac Inn on Saranac Lake in New York State. Perfectly restored, she is now owned by a Michigan sportsman and boat collector.*

The greatest of them all was *Baby Bootlegger*. She was designed by George Crouch and built by Henry Nevins for the 1924 Gold Cup. Another bit of good news is that she's still around; her hull and her Hispano-Suiza V8 were restored by Mark Mason and his New England Boat and Motor team in the 1980s. Photographs of *Bootlegger* show an extraordinary tube of mahogany with a subtle waterline stripe of contrasting wood. The heads of the sixty thousand bronze screws that fasten her planking glow under multiple coats of varnish, and altogether *Bootlegger* displays an otherworldly beauty that no other powerboat in the world can claim. Always a lucky boat, she won the Gold Cup in 1924 and 1925, the first time after a second-place finish and disqualification of the leader for an infraction of the new rules. Other raceboats and pleasure boats adopted the rounded-sheerline style of this boat—notably Crouch's *Teaser* of 1924, John Hacker's *Scotty* of 1929, and Canada's Greavette Streamliner runabouts—but none had the elegance or élan of *Bootlegger*.

By the end of the 1920s, there were at least a dozen builders of mahogany runabouts in the United States and Canada, and there were contests for a variety of inboard and outboard classes of boats that were built for speed alone. Among the racers were 151-class boats, single-cockpit speedboats restricted to small engines of no more than 151 cubic inches. *Miss Daytona*, shown here, is an outstanding example of a 151 machine and also proof of how competitive speedboat building and racing had become by 1929. *Miss Daytona* is a sixteen-foot-five-inch (5m) step-bottomed boat that is powered by one of Harry Miller's supercharged 151-cubic-inch fours. This little engine can deliver 250 horsepower on 115-octane racing fuel, and is the ancestor of Miller's legendary Indianapolis 500 race-car engines. By the end of the 1920s, the mahogany runabout had grown to examples bigger than thirty feet (9.1m). Some of them were the playthings of the rich, while others were in service at resorts, where tourists boarded them for "thrill rides" that scared them half to death. By the end of the 1920s, a big thirty-foot (9.1m) HackerCraft would do better than forty miles per hour (64kph) with an unmodified engine.

In the 1930s, the mahogany runabout experienced several transformations, much as the automobile did during that Depression decade, when, whether or not the rich got richer while the poor got poorer, two extremes of means and style appeared in the world of vehicles. The 1930s were a great decade of luxury automobiles, many of them custom-built, but the era brought economic distress to most people. At the lower end of the market, both boatbuilders and automobile manufacturers struggled to survive on sales of products cheap enough for the public to afford. Chris-Craft went from forty models in production in 1931 to only seven in 1932–33, all of them modest runabouts and utility boats priced as low as $500. The boat so much admired in the 1981 film *On Golden Pond* was one of the plain-vanilla Chris-Craft utilities from the 1930s. Other boatbuilders followed Chris-Craft's lead,

*B*aby Bootlegger *was built to win the 1924 Gold Cup powerboat race, which she did by a fluke. She won with no controversy in 1925. Designer George Crouch gave her extraordinary aesthetics, and current owner Mark Mason gave her an extraordinary restoration in the 1980s.*

but many remained upscale and somehow survived the Great Depression. HackerCraft, Gar Wood, Robinson Seagull, and the elite Canadian boat shops, among others, continued to produce great boats for the few who could afford them.

The essential style of the mahogany runabout remained the perfect idea it had been during the 1920s, but in the 1930s and on into the 1940s, speedboats became even more stylish. Gar Wood began to produce "sedan" versions of his runabouts with rakish mahogany day cabins. *Lizzie*, shown here, is a good and rare example of the type—and also a boat with the sweeping lines and rounded edges of 1930s streamlining. Into the 1940s and 1950s, speedboats adopted many of the stylistic features

of automobiles, including rounded bows in imitation of bullnose cars, as well as chrome trim, sometimes too much of it. When it was done just right, the extra touch of styling produced wonderful blends of warm varnished wood and cool metal. Some excellent examples of this include John Hacker's 1940s and 1950s custom runabouts and Chris-Craft's Cobras and nineteen-foot (5.7m) Racing Runabouts.

By the 1960s, only a few builders of mahogany speedboats remained, principally Chris-Craft and Century. Both had survived the Great Depression, World War II, and a postwar sorting-out that had seen Gar Wood and HackerCraft, among others, close their doors. Neither Chris-Craft nor Century, builders of varnished-wood speedboats, was likely to survive fiberglass unless they adopted the new material and remained competitive with upstart builders of plastic boats. The new fiberglass boats were cheaper than boats hand-built of wood, many of them looked like floating automobiles, and they were advertised as maintenance-free. In the early 1960s, Chris-Craft and Century were already building flashy plastic speedboats instead of flashy mahogany speed-

boats, and by the end of the decade both builders had launched their last mahogany runabouts, Century in 1965 and Chris-Craft in 1968. It was the end of an era.

Meanwhile, on Lago d'Iseo in Italy, after the war, the mahogany runabout began a European era of elite speed-boating that would last for forty-five years and produce boats admired all over the world for their elegance and perfection of finish. In 1950, Carlo Riva and Gino

No speedboat builders in the world ever surpassed the Canadians, whose boats are perfect in line, detail, craftsmanship, finish, and pure style. This twenty-four-foot (7.3m) Minett runabout from 1924 is a perfect example of their work.

The automobile influence was as good for most wooden boats as it was bad for most fiberglass boats. This Chris-Craft Cobra is a rare and wonderful mahogany boat with a fiberglass fin decorating its after deck. The Cobras came along in the mid-1950s.

Gervasoni began to build two Honduras mahogany speedboats a month in the Riva family's old boatyard on the lake. The fame of these boats spread from the lake district to the Italian Riviera, then to the French Riviera and Monaco. By the middle of the 1950s, fleets of Rivas were docked side by side in the holiday ports of the Mediterranean. Riva's big and shapely twenty-nine-foot (8.8m) Aquarama is described by the builder as "a precious mahogany sculpture," and the photographs in these

pages will testify to the truth of the claim. These elite machines—with twin 350-horsepower V8 engines, leather upholstery, a sunbathing space over the engine compartment, and two berths under the foredeck—are literally wood sculptures. Since 1954, they have been made with mahogany veneer molded to the shape of the hull. Riva built the Aquaramas, as well as a changing fleet of smaller models, for customers all over the world until the end of 1995, when the last seven Aquaramas were

The 1950s also brought the dazzling Rivas to the waterfronts of Europe. These elite boats were American-style mahogany runabouts reinvented by the Italians with more sculptural lines and with the leather upholstery and precise engineering of Italian sports cars.

delivered to various oil sheiks and European millionaires. It was the end of another era.

New speedboats continue to be launched, many of them the replicas considered in the next chapter of this book. Others are new variations on the theme. A recent launching is William Garden's design for a twenty-four-foot (7.3m) mahogany speedboat with more vee shape in its bottom and greater width, qualities that will give it better behavior in coastal waters. Garden's blue-bottomed runabout, with small cockpits fore and aft, is a variation on the gentlemen's raceboats that competed for the Gold Cup in the Roaring Twenties.

Since they first appeared eighty years ago, classic speedboats seem to have survived quite nicely through all the many changes in the boating world, and they seem to have survived with very little change. That is a large part of what makes them classic. One of Mr. Webster's definitions of the word is "in accordance with a coherent system considered as having its parts perfectly coordinated to their purpose." Classic speedboats are that—and much more.

Note: Sources for plans, patterns, kits, and completed boats are given in an appendix at the back of the book.

CHAPTER 8

Replicas

Tales of great old boats discovered in barns, chicken coops, and the boathouses of abandoned camps in the Adirondacks are part of the folklore of the old-boat hobby. You still hear such tales—and even sagas of detective work in tracking down a particular disappeared boat—but there are fewer all the time. There are also fewer desirable old boats all the time. The old-boat and wooden-boat enthusiasm has now discovered most of the easy restorations, for example, the speedboat that was only used one season and then stored for fifty years in a dry place. The hobby has moved on to wrecks and even to what the hobbyists describe as basket cases. There is now considerable pride taken in the perfect restoration of a boat discovered in a farmer's field with large holes in its bottom and all its hardware missing. As with the automobile-restoration hobby, there is now a minor industry in replica parts.

There are also replica boats. Some of these are true replicas—i.e., exact copies. Others are sort-of copies, and still others are contempo-rary interpretations or adaptations of old designs. I will use "replica" here in a very broad sense that takes in most of these categories. Some replicas are historic, such as the single re-creation of an important ves-sel, and some are new copies of an historic type. The approximation of the Pilgrims' *Mayflower* at Plymouth, Massachusetts, and Mystic Seaport Museum's exact re-creation of a Crosby catboat, shown on page 82, both fit this category. Other replicas, also normally single-boat projects, are built for customers who admire a particular boat from the past and know that they will never find an original. Classic sailboats and classic speedboat re-creations fit this category, and there have been some great ones in recent years. A final replica category is the new boat that either looks like or is identical to a great old boat and is produced in some quantity. Many of these replicas are fiberglass, but some are wood, and they must be wood to be proper re-creations of the wooden-boat past.

Pages 110 and 111:
Details of Bill Morgan's replica of
the 1920s and 1930s Gold Cup
raceboat El Legarto.

Right:
A crew of twentieth-
century rowers in a replica of an
eighteenth-century boat—one of
Pacific Challenge's growing fleet of
replica gigs and ship's boats from the
era of Cook and Vancouver.

The Atlantic Challenge rowing and sailing gigs shown at left are replicas of a late-eighteenth century French warship's boat. Copies of this boat have been built all over the world with the help of Atlantic Challenge, and they compete in a sort of nautical Olympics.

New copies of Whitehall boats, Rangeley Lakes boats, other nineteenth-century classics, and even new cedar-and-canvas canoes are all more or less replicas, but two faithful resurrections of eighteenth-century small boats are worthy of note. The first is the 1790s ship's boat built by the Northwest School of Wooden Boatbuilding for the Jefferson County Maritime Commission and the Wooden Boat Foundation in Port Townsend, Washington; the second is Lance Lee's fleet of thirty-eight-foot (11.7m) rowing/sailing gigs. Lee's gigs are copies of a French warship's boat that turned up in Ireland in 1796 and is now in Dublin's National Maritime Museum. Lee's boats are also elegant ancestors of the Whitehalls, and even the much-evolved college rowing shells, which begin their history in 1829 with Oxford's

forty-five-foot (13.7m) and 2,434-pound (1,105kg) Eight. Lance Lee and his Apprenticeshop and Atlantic Challenge crews in Maine have built five of the gigs; others have been built in Ireland, Wales, Canada, Denmark, France, and Russia; and more are in the works in Mexico, Ireland, France, Canada, the United States, and Tasmania. This boom in replicas of eighteenth-century rowing boats is due to Lance Lee's Atlantic Challenge Foundation, which gets these boats built for goals larger than simply bringing back a great little vessel from two hundred years ago. All are vehicles for the Atlantic Challenge rowing program, which teaches youngsters pride, craftsmanship, and teamwork as they build, use, and maintain these boats in their home waters. Atlantic Challenge also organizes international competitions in

G*rand-Craft builds new copies of classic speedboats that represent types and styles dating from the 1920s to the 1950s. Right: A twenty-seven-foot (8.2m) Grand-Craft runabout that is reminiscent of the square-windshield Chris-Crafts of the 1920s.*

Below:
A *detail of windshield hardware, showing the authenticity of these re-creations of past styles.*

the gigs at events like Operation Sail and the big traditional-boat gatherings in France.

Thanks to the impetus of Gray's Harbor Historical Seaport of Aberdeen, Washington, and its Pacific Challenge, something similar has been happening in the Pacific Northwest of the United States and Canada. The Pacific Challenge involves contests in rowing, sail-handling, and seamanship among historic small craft and replicas of eighteenth-century ship's boats and gigs. Pacific Challenges take place in late spring in a new location every year. The Challenges even include a contest in bottom-sounding and chart-making, tasks that the crews

undertook in the ship's boats carried by Vancouver, Cook, and other explorers. The Wooden Boat Foundation's replica ship's boat is based on one of the boats George Vancouver carried aboard HMS *Discovery* from 1792 to 1795. The replica is a heavy knockaround rowboat/sailboat that weighs a ton (0.9t) and is twenty-five feet eight inches long (7.8m) with a six-foot-eight-inch (2m) beam and a two-foot-one-inch (63.5cm) draft. This replica gives us a look at what small craft were like before the many changes of the nineteenth century.

These days, the largest category of replica wooden boats is the brand-new speedboat or raceboat that brings back the 1920–1960 era of varnished mahogany and pleated leather. The largest fleet of these boats has come out the doors of a Holland, Michigan, factory with a sign on the building that reads "Grand-Craft." Holland is an old boatbuilding and furniture town where Chris-Crafts were once built. In the early 1980s, Grand-Craft began to build replicas of Chris-Craft's 1930 square-windshield, twenty-four-foot (7.3m) runabout, delivering a new mahogany speedboat with modern machinery and a modified bottom design that was at least as good as the original. The boat was a stunning success. The Grand-Craft fleet now includes fifteen boats, from a twenty-foot (6m)

double-cockpit runabout to a thirty-six-foot (11m) commuter cruiser, a range of models and sizes similar to Chris-Craft's production in the late 1920s. These boats are hand-built in the mahogany-runabout tradition. They are admirably true to the lines and finish of the old boats, and they represent runabout and cruiser types and styles from the 1920s, 1930s, and 1950s. Grand-Craft declines to call them replicas; they are "new wooden boats based on old models," says the company president. As the photographs in these pages show, they are wonderful new old boats.

Two other notable series-production builders of all-new classic mahogany runabouts are the Turcotte brothers' Gar Wood Boat Company on the Hudson River and Bill Morgan's Hacker Boat Company on Lake George. Both are located in old-boat regions of New York State, and both are devoted to resurrecting the products and the cachet of great old names in the speedboat game. Except for their modern engines, the new Gar Woods are exactly like the old, from their chrome-plated cutwaters to their vee windshields to the contrasting dark-and-light wood on their decks. The Turcottes currently build replicas of Gar Wood classics in sixteen-foot (4.8m), eighteen-foot (5.4m), twenty-two-foot (6.7m), twenty-five-foot (7.6m), thirty-three-foot (10m), and forty-foot (12.1m) lengths. The fleet includes copies of the single-cockpit sixteen-foot (4.8m) Gar Wood Speedster and a thirty-three-foot (10m) Baby Gar with single or twin V8 engines.

Bill Morgan's Hacker Boat Company builds a large variety of John Hacker designs for racing machines, clas-

Another Grand-Craft replica, this thirty-five-foot (9.1m) commuter with forward cockpit, day cabin amidships, and mahogany-runabout lines is reminiscent of the Chris-Craft and Robinson Seagull commuters of the 1920s and 1930s.

A single-cockpit "gentleman's runabout," the original El Legarto was designed and built in 1921 by the legendary John Hacker for joyrides, not racing. Converted to a raceboat, she won the Gold Cup in 1933, 1934, and 1935. Bill Morgan's twenty-seven-foot (8.2m) replica, shown here, is faithful to the original except for power. The new boat has a three-hundred-horsepower Chrysler Hemi for speeds of seventy miles per hour (112kph).

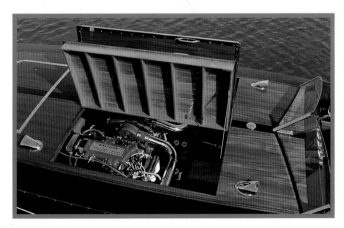

pointing out that his boats represent contemporary improvements to structure and durability, even though they are pretty much true to the original designs. He makes a different claim: "We feel we're a re-creation of the Hacker Boat Company."

Two series-built boats based on the legendary racing machines of the 1920s are Van Dam WoodCraft's thirty-five-foot (10.6m) Stogie and Zebcraft's twenty-four-foot (7.3m) single-step hydroplane. Both are stylish approximations of the old Gold Cup contenders, although the Zebcraft's twenty-four-foot (7.3m) length and stepped bottom would have brought disqualification from the gentlemen's runabout races of the Jazz Age. Both are slim mahogany bullets with single cockpits and appropriate

sic runabouts, utilities, and even commuters. The company uses some newer items of hardware as well as modern adhesives, building techniques, and engines. However, the boats have the same Honduras mahogany and visible fittings that Hacker himself used in the 1920s, 1930s, and 1940s. Bill Morgan sidesteps the "replica" issue too,

Above:

*T*he thirty-five-foot (10.7m) Stogie from Van Dam WoodCraft is a long, slim approximation of the Gold Cup boats of the 1920s and 1930s.

Left:

*P*owered by a pair of big new V8s, Stogie is capable of speeds of more than sixty miles per hour (96kph).

Ken Bassett's fifteen-foot (4.5m) Rascal, shown here doing fifty miles per hour (80kph) and handling like a Jaguar XK-120, is a stylish outboard replica.

period hardware. The Zebcraft, powered by a tweaked Chevrolet V8, will do seventy miles per hour (112kph). The Stogie is a thirty-five-foot by seven-feet-four-inch (10.6 by 2.2m) double-ender powered by a pair of four-hundred-horsepower V8s. This boat will exceed sixty miles per hour (96kph) and look like the 1927 Gold Cup in the process. A second boat from Zebcraft is a twenty-six-footer (8m) with pleated seating for five passengers.

Two re-creations of classic outboards are Simon Fletcher's several little Speedliners and Ken Bassett's Rascal, a clever re-creation of a 1930s single-cockpit sport boat. The Speedliner reproductions are close approximations of the boats built between 1946 and 1961 by a Missouri company that produced outboard racing boats and mahogany outboard sport boats. Fletcher Boats builds its Speedliner copies in thirteen- to eighteen-foot

(4 to 5.4m) lengths. The boats have Naugahyde upholstery, hulls of Bruynzeel mahogany marine plywood over oak frames, and laid mahogany decks with white caulking lines and ten coats of varnish. The thirteen-foot (4m) Fletcher/Speedliner hybrid is a fifty-horsepower jet boat. The eighteen-footer (5.4m) is an inboard powered by a 140-horsepower Volvo engine.

A similar concept, Ken Bassett's fifteen-foot (4.5m) Rascal is handmade from Bruynzeel mahogany marine plywood and solid Honduras mahogany, and its double-planking scheme has the solid mahogany on the deck and on the outside of the bright-finished hull. Frames are spruce, and the hull's extra strength and stiffness are the result of laminating the mahogany-plywood inner hull and solid-mahogany outer hull together with epoxy. This boat, with plumb bow, chrome cutwater, chrome trim, and a single cockpit behind a vee windshield, is reminiscent of Century Thunderbolts and other small sport boats of the 1930s. With a stock sixty-horsepower outboard, it can hit fifty-two miles per hour (83.2kph), and the builder compares its handling qualities to those of classic English sports cars.

Something more sedate in a replica powerboat is the twenty-three-foot (7m) *Hunter Cabin Launch* supplied as a kit or custom-complete from Pat Spurlock's Elliott Bay Steam Launch Co. in Portland, Oregon. Like thousands of originals built at the turn of the last century, the boat pictured is a "steam" hull but with a "one-lung" engine. Cabins were added to launches just as soon as the heat and space required for a boiler could be eliminated. This 1905 design sleeps four and slides along at eight miles per hour (12.8kph) burning less than one quart as a diesel, or, 3.29 hp (68 amps @ 36 volts @ 2.45 kw) as an electric. Surviving steam and hunter cabin launches are rare, and replicas in wood and fiberglass are a phenomenon of the past thirty years.

Equally rare, and especially desirable, are Gold Cup raceboats from the 1920s and 1930s. Several spectacular replicas have been built in recent years for the few who could afford them. The two in these pages are Ken Bassett's re-creation of *Miss Minneapolis,* a boat originally designed and built by Chris "Chris-Craft" Smith, and Mark Mason's new copy of *Miss Columbia.* The original *Miss Minneapolis* was sponsored by the Minneapolis Athletic Club. The boat was powered by a 250-horse-

power Sterling engine and won the Gold Cup in 1916. Ken Bassett's 1990 *Miss Minneapolis,* built for a Florida sportsman, is a twenty- by six-foot (6 by 1.8m) mahogany hull that can reach scary speeds powered by a sixteen-cylinder, 585-horsepower engine that was carefully engineered from two 350-cubic-inch V8s connected together.

Miss Columbia is a replica of one of the great gentlemen's runabouts that contended for the Gold Cup

A hunter-cabin launch from Elliott Bay Steam Launch Company—this one diesel-powered—decorates a backwater of Desolation Sound, British Columbia, Canada.

Right:
Built in 1986, this single-cockpit speedboat is a replica of Miss Columbia, a Gold Cup raceboat fielded in 1924. This replica was built by Bill Cooper under contract to New England Boat and Motor, and her powerplant is a 1920s Packard Gold Cup Six.

Right, below:
An earlier Gold Cup boat in a recent replication—Ken Bassett's approximation of the mighty Miss Minneapolis of 1916.

in the 1920s. Designed by George Crouch and built by Henry Nevins for members of New York City's Columbia Yacht Club, the original *Miss Columbia* came close but never won the Gold Cup during a racing career that began in 1924 and lasted into the 1930s. Nevertheless, she was just what a gentleman's runabout was supposed to be: beautiful, powerful, and well-behaved. The replica, equally beautiful, powerful, and well-behaved, was built in 1986 by the Bill Cooper boat shop of Sippewisset, Massachusetts. The project was organized by Mark Mason and his New England Boat and Motor team for a legendary Thousand Islands sportsman and boat collector. The replica is powered by a six-cylinder, 400-horsepower Packard Gold Cup engine, a duplicate of the powerplant that was put into the original in 1925 to replace a Hispano-Suiza.

Replicas of classic sailboats, like their originals, are nearly all custom creations—single-boat projects that resurrect something wonderful or historic that has been gone for decades. The Herreshoff Buzzards Bay 25s are not gone. All four of the originals are still sailing in New England, but their owners have refused to part with them at any price. Because of this, several replicas have been built as tributes to the beauty and good behavior of these thirty-two-foot (9.7m) day boats. A 1995 re-creation of the Buzzards Bay 25 was built by Joel White's Brooklin Boatyard in Brooklin, Maine.

Another Maine-built re-creation of the past is a sandbagger built in 1990 by the Rockport Apprenticeshop (now The Artisans College) in Rockport, Maine, based on an 1860 boat called *Comet,* that was designed by A. Cary Smith. The sandbaggers competed from the 1850s to the 1890s, mostly in New York Harbor and Long Island Sound. These were pure racing machines whose enor-

*B*elow, a fiberglass replica of Nathanael Herreshoff's Fish Class sloop is at her mooring in a New England harbor. Varnished-oak trim matches that of the original boats. One of the wood originals is shown on page 33.

mous expanses of sail and relatively flat bottoms required crews of Bowery boys to shift sandbags from one side of the boat to the other to keep them from capsizing while being sailed. Each sandbag weighed as much as seventy-five pounds (34kg), and we can guess that the weights of the crew members were in proportion. During the Gilded Age, these wild performers brought years of excitement to spectators on shore and aboard excursion steamers. The excitement was enhanced by large cash wagers, plenty of controversy, practically no racing rules, and an occasional fistfight. The eighteen-foot-two-inch (5.5m) replica was built for a sailor on Buzzards Bay, who describes her as the most demanding boat he's ever sailed. Only a few of the original sandbaggers are still around, and four of them

are in maritime museums. If you want one, you have to build it yourself or have it built—a thing the racing sailors of the second half of the nineteenth century thought nothing of doing in backyards, lumberyards, and shops that specialized in small boats and small yachts.

Since the 1980s, professional shops and amateur craftsmen have built replicas, re-creations, and reinterpretations of traditional small boats, classic wooden cruisers and speedboats, legendary race boats, elegant old racing and cruising sailboats, and even wooden canoes and kayaks from the early years of the twentieth century. A large part of the future of wooden-boat enjoyment and appreciation will be these replications, reproductions, and reinterpretations of boats from the past. An era ended during the 1960s when new launchings of wooden boats declined sharply and mass-produced fiberglass boats quickly came to dominate the market. In the 1970s and 1980s, a new era began when old-boat hobbyists and sportsmen, frustrated by the dearth of great old boats left to find or restore, asked themselves a creative question: "Why not just build a new one?" Many new old boats have been built since then, and it seems safe to predict that the wooden boats of the future will represent more and more of these admirable re-creations of the wooden boat past.

Note: Sources for plans, patterns, kits, and completed boats are given in an appendix at the back of the book.

Only a few sandbaggers from the last half of the nineteenth century have survived. If you want one of these exciting boats, you have to build a new one. This boat, built in 1990 at Maine's Artisans College, is a replica of one of the eighteen-foot (5.5m) sandbaggers from the 1860s.

Sources

Following is a list of addresses for boatbuilders, boat designers, wooden-boat and traditional-boat publications, and sources for wooden-boat plans and kits.

UNITED STATES

The Adirondack Museum
Plans Office
P.O. Box 99
Blue Mountain Lake, NY 12812

John G. Alden
Yacht Design and Yacht Brokerage
89 Commercial Wharf
Boston, MA 02110

Alden Ocean Shells
167½ Main Street
Box 368
Eliot, ME 03903

The Apprenticeshop of Rockland
P.O. Box B
Rockland, ME 04841

The Artisan's College
P.O. Box 539
Rockport, ME 04856

John Atkin
Boat and Yacht Design
P.O. Box 3005
Noroton, CT 06820

Atlantic Challenge
P.O. Box B
Rockland, ME 04841

Ken Bassett, boatbuilder
Blockhouse Point
P.O. Box 136A
North Hero, VT 05474

Jay Benford Boat Plans
Box 477A
St. Michaels, MD 21663

Benjamin River Marine
Route 175
Brooklin, ME 04616

Bill Cooper Boat Shop
267 Sippewisset Road
Falmouth, MA 02540

Boatbuilder: The Journal of Boat
Design and Construction
P.O. Box 540638
Merritt Island, FL 32954

Boatbuilder Magazine
P.O. Box 2626
Greenwich, CT 06836

Boat Design Quarterly
P.O. Box 98
Brooklin, ME 04616

BOATHOUSE Press
6744 S.E. 36th Avenue
Portland, OR 97202

Philip C. Bolger, boat designer
29 Ferry Street
Gloucester, MA 01930

Brooklin Boat Yard
Center Harbor Road
Brooklin, ME 04616

Clark Craft Boat Plans
16-42 Aqualane
Tonowanda, NY 14150

Classic Boating Magazine
280 Lac La Belle Drive
Oconomowoc, WI 53066

Common Sense Boat Designs
11765 S.W. Ebberts Court
Beaverton, OR 97005

Data Boat International
Boat Plans
P.O. Box A
Bellingham, WA 98227

Elco
16 Shadyside Road
Ramsey, NJ 07466

Eldredge-McInnis
Yacht Design and Yacht Brokerage
P.O. Box F
Hingham, MA 02043

Elliott Bay Steam Launch
Company
6744 S.E. 36th Avenue
Portland, OR 97202

Ellis Yacht Brokerage
P.O. Box 265
Manset, ME 04679

Fletcher Boats
292 Wellman Road
Port Angeles, WA 98363

Flounder Bay Boat
Lumber Co., Inc.
1019 Third Street
Anacortes, WA 98221

Freedom Boatworks
P.O. Box 511
Baraboo, WI 53913

Gar Wood Boat Company
129 Columbia Street
Cohoes, NY 12047

Geodesic Airolite Boats
c/o Monfort Associates
R.R. 2, Box 416W
Wiscasset, ME 04578

Glen-L Marine Designs
9152 Rosecrans Avenue
Bellflower, CA 90706

Grand Craft
430 West 21st Street
Holland, MI 49423

Hacker Boat Company
P.O. Box 2576
Silver Bay, NY 12874

Tom Hill, boatbuilder
166 Ferguson Avenue
Burlington, VT 05401

Hodgdon Brothers Yachtbuilders
Murray Hill Road
East Boothbay, ME 04544

Huckins Yacht Corporation
3482 Lakeshore Boulevard
Jacksonville, FL 32210

Independence Seaport Museum
Penn's Landing
211 South Columbus Boulevard
at Walnut Street
Philadelphia, PA 19106

Instant Boats
H.H. Payson & Co.
Pleasant Beach Road
South Thomaston, ME 04858

International Yacht Restoration
    School
28 Church Street
Newport, RI 02840

Steve Kaulback, boatbuilder
P.O. Box 144
Charlotte, VT 05445

Lowell's Boat Shop
459 Main Street
Amesbury, MA 01913

Boyd Mefferd
Launch and Runabout Brokerage
P.O. Box 9
Canton, CT 06019

Messing About in Boats Magazine
29 Burley Street
Wenham, MA 01984

Monfort Associates
R.R. 2, Box 416W
Wiscasset, ME 04578

Mystic Seaport Museum
Boat Plans Archive
75 Greenmanville Avenue
Mystic, CT 06355

New England Boat and Motor
P.O. Box 1283
Laconia, NH 03247

Northwest School of Wooden
    Boatbuilding
251 West Otto Street
Port Townsend, WA 98368

Mike O'Brien, boat designer
c/o *WoodenBoat Magazine*
Naskeag Road
Brooklin, ME 04616

Onion River Boatworks
Blockhouse Point
Box 136A
North Hero, VT 05474

Harold "Dynamite" Payson,
    boatbuilder
Pleasant Beach Road
South Thomaston, ME 04858

Pete Culler Boat Plans
c/o George Kelley
22 Lookout Lane
Hyannis, MA 02601

RKL Boatworks
P.O. Box W30
Mount Desert, ME 04660

Robert H. Baker Boat Plans
c/o A.W. Baker
29 Drift Road
Westport, MA 02790

Rybovich/Spencer
4200 Poinsettia Avenue
West Palm Beach, FL 33407

Sid-Craft Boats
102 Commerce Drive
Montgomeryville, PA 18936

Speedliner
292 Wellman Road
Port Angeles, WA 98363

Steve Redmond Boat Plans
c/o T. Miliano
P.O. Box 35177
Sarasota, FL 34242

Stimson Marine Boat Plans
River Road
R.R. 1, Box 524
Boothbay, ME 04537

Van Dam Wood Craft
970 East Division Street
Boyne City, MI 49712

The Wooden Boat Foundation
380 Jefferson Street
Port Townsend, WA 98368

WoodenBoat Magazine
Naskeag Road
Brooklin, ME 04616

The WoodenBoat Store
P.O. Box 78
Brooklin, ME 04616

Joel White, boat designer
    and boatbuilder
Brooklin Boatyard
Center Harbor Road
Brooklin, ME 04616

Zebcraft
RFD #1, Box 312
Ashland, NH 03217

CANADA

Alder Bay Boat Co.
1247 Cartwright Street
Vancouver, BC V6H 3R8

Bent Jesperson Boatbuilders Ltd.
10995 Madrona Dr., RR#2
Sidney, BC V8L 3R9

Gil Bibby Boatbuilding
151 Hendershott Road
Hannon, ON L0R 1P0

Clarion Boats
1155 N. Service Road West
Suite 11
Oakville, ON L6M 3E3

Covey Island Boatworks Ltd.
Petite Riviere, NS B0J 2P0

The Dory Shop
Box 1678
Lunenburg, NS B0J 2C0

William Garden
P.O. Box 2371
Sidney, BC V8L 3Y3

Clarence R. Heisler & Son Ltd.
Indian Point, RR#2
Mahone Bay, NS B0J 2E0

K Squared Areomarine
    Woodworks
4851 Elgin Street
Vancouver, BC V5V 4S2

LaHave Marine Woodworking
P.O. Box 144
LaHave, NS B0R 1C0

Peter London
2220 Harbour Road
Sidney, BC V8L 2P6

Ludlow Boatworks
RR#4
Kemptville, ON K0G 1J0

McQueen Boatworks Ltd.
11571 Twigg Place
Richmond, BC V6V 2K7

Millar-Potter Boat Restoration
P.O. Box 56
Manotick, ON K4M 1A2

New Dublin Watercraft
RR#1, LaHave (Dublin Shore)
Lunenburg County, NS
B0R 1C0

Nova Scotia Community
College
Lunenburg Campus,
75 High Street
Bridgewater, NS B4V 1V8

NW Historic Watercraft
Whaler Bay
Galiano Island, BC V0N 1P0

Port Dover Boatworks
River Drive
Port Dover, ON N0A 1N0

Service Maritime Independant
2145 Du Tremblay
Longeuil, PQ J4N 1A9

Slaunwhite's Boat & Joinery
Shop
RR#1, Mader's Cove
Mahone Bay, NS B0J 2E0

Steven's Boatworks
P.O. Box 2, Western Shore
Lunenburg, NS B0J 3M0

The Tender Craft Boatshop Inc.
284 Brock Avenue
Toronto, ON M6K 2M4

Virgin Forest Boatworks
42 6th Street NE
Calgary, AB T2E 3X9

Winard Wood Ltd.
10563 McDonald Park Road
Sidney, BC V8L 3J3

UNITED KINGDOM

Classic Boat Magazine and
The Boatman
Link House
Dingwell Avenue
Croydon, Surrey
England
CR9 2TA

Iain Oughtred, boat designer
Gorton House Cottage
Lasswade, Edinburgh
Scotland EH18 1EH

FRANCE

Chasse-Marée Magazine
B.P. 159
29177 Douarnenez Cedex
France

ITALY

Riva
SPA Via Predore #30
24067 Sarnico, Lombardia
Italia

Photography Credits

Armstrong and Roberts:
© Marty Loken: 2, 42
Courtesy the Artisan's College
Archive: 5, 122–123
© Ken Bassett: 120 bottom
© Paul Bouchey: 50
© Alan C. Brown: 47
© Jim Brown: 27 bottom, 43, 44,
45 both, 54, 55, 56, 72 right,
73, 75 both, 87, 92 top, 106
both
© Polly Brown: 105, 118, 120
top
Courtesy Richard Butz: 64
© Christopher Cunningham: 70,
71, 72 left
© Robert Bruce Duncan: 8, 100,
102 bottom, 104

Courtesy Elliot Bay Steam
Launch Co.: 88, 119
© William B. Folsom: 12
Courtesy Douglas Fowler/
Photography by David
Brumsted: 48–49 both
Courtesy Freedom Boat Works:
98
© Benjamin Fuller: 46, 51
© Dale Gamble: 84 both
Courtesy Glen-L: 65
Courtesy Grand Craft: 114 both
Courtesy Tom Hill/ Photography
by Michael Weizenegger:
59 top, 60
Leo de Wys: © Vladpans: 16
© Neal and Molly Jansen: 22
© Lance Lee: 38–39, 113

© Benjamin Mendlowitz: 59 bottom, 81 right, 91, 96
Courtesy Michael McMenemy:
61
Courtesy Monfort Associates:
68, 69 bottom; Photography
by Peter Jones: 69 top
© Mystic Seaport Photo: 52
bottom, 82, 89, 95
© Dan Nerney: 52 top, 80, 97
Stock Newport: © Alison
Langley: 33, 78, 83, 99
bottom; © Peter McGowan:
53; © Gary John Norman:
24 © Onne Van Der Wal: 27
top, 35, 79, 109, 122
© Art Paine: 10, 11 both, 21,
30–31, 34, 94

© J.H. Peterson: 3, 76, 77
© Neil Rabinowitz: 13, 17, 18,
23, 26, 28, 31, 74, 86, 92
bottom, 99 top, 102 top,
112, 115
© Carol Simowitz: 14–15, 29
© Ed Simpson: 20
© Sherry Streeter: 58
Courtesy Van Dam WoodCraft/
Photography by G. Randall
Goss: 117 both
© Norm Wangard: 90, 107
© Alan Weitz: 6, 36, 37, 57, 62,
63, 66, 67, 81 bottom, 85,
93, 101, 103, 108, 110, 111,
116, 121
© Dudley Witney: 9, 19, 32, 25
© Ken Woisard: 40, 41

Index